30 years of Shire Publications

A bibliography for collectors 1962-91

Contents

First published 1992. ISBN 0 7478 0170 3.

Printed in Great Britain by C. I. Thomas & Sons (Haverfordwest) Ltd, Press Buildings, Merlins Bridge, Haverfordwest, Dyfed SA61 1XF.

INTRODUCTION

This is a bibliography of books published by Shire Publications in the thirty years since it was founded in 1962 and the twenty-five years since full-time book publishing began in 1967. Shire's various paperback series are now being increasingly collected and this list has been published to help those who wish to assemble complete series.

In 1962 the trading name Shire Publications was suggested by John Hinton for the publication of a brief guide to the Suffolk coast to be called *Discovering East Suffolk*. The two partners in the venture were John Hinton and John Rotheroe, both in full-time jobs in advertising in London.

Discovering East Suffolk was conceived as a 24 page book describing the county through a series of five motoring routes and a gazetteer of the main towns and villages. Although nominally priced at one shilling and sixpence, it was to be given away to visitors via coach operators, petrol stations, local churches and tourist information points. The revenue was to come from advertisements which took the form of seventy-word entries in the gazetteer, describing hotels, restaurants, shops and other commercial establishments.

Shire Publications was registered as a business name at Holly Lodge, Marlesford, Woodbridge, Suffolk, and a brochure was sent to prospective advertisers. Mary Gurry, who lived in Woodbridge, agreed to help sell the advertising and act as local manager.

The Shire tree logo was designed by a colleague, Stuart Herriott-Smith, who also drew the windmill illustration for the cover of *Discovering East Suffolk*. John Rotheroe wrote the text. (The Shire tree logo was redesigned by Felix Partridge in 1969.)

The covers and the sheets of the text pages for ten thousand copies of *Discovering East Suffolk* were printed in Holborn by The Norman Press. They were then folded, gathered and stapled by hand to save costs and returned to the printers for trimming. Finished copies were distributed free throughout east Suffolk during the summer of 1962.

In 1963 a second edition of ten thousand copies was printed, this time with a foreword by Suffolk author Simon Dewes and contributions from W. G. Arnott and R. A. Campbell. Again it was distributed free. In neither edition was advertising revenue sufficient to cover costs and both made a loss. John Hinton decided to leave the venture and was replaced as partner by Jacqueline Rotheroe. A third edition of *Discovering East Suffolk* was published in July 1964 and was sold through bookshops.

In 1964 Shire Publications moved to Gubblecote Cross, Tring, Hertfordshire, and a second title, *Discovering Ipswich*, was published. Written by Jacqueline Rotheroe, 500 copies were hand-printed on an Adana platen machine. A further 1500 copies were printed commercially by Enta Print. In 1965 *Discovering Norfolk* was published using the same windmill cover design as *Discovering East Suffolk*. A fourth edition of *Discovering East Suffolk* was published, printed by Progress Press in Malta.

In March 1966 John Rotheroe resigned from his job and with his wife Jacqueline formed Bucks Life Limited, registered in Aylesbury, to publish a monthly county magazine about Buckinghamshire. The magazine attracted contributions from a number of authors and illustrators and one of them, Liz Tresilian, was asked to write *Discovering Wiltshire*. Published in May 1967, this was followed by *Discovering Castle Combe* by the same author, *Discovering Buckinghamshire* by Cadbury Lamb, *Discovering West Suffolk* by John Rotheroe and *Discovering the Chilterns* by J. H. B. Peel.

In August 1967 *Discovering Brasses* was published. This was a guide to rubbing church memorial brasses, written by Malcolm Cook, who had written an article on the subject for

Bucks Life. It was an immediate success and was reprinted within three months. As a consequence John Rotheroe commissioned other *Bucks Life* authors to write for the 'Discovering' series and in 1968 a further 36 titles were published.

The ideas for many of the titles, and a number of the texts, came from Margaret Baker, a reference librarian who knew what gaps there were in available published material. Historian John Kinross, who had been the first author to send in an unsolicited article to *Bucks Life*, wrote *Discovering Battlefields in Southern England*, the first of the 1968 titles, and subsequently wrote others on battlefields and castles.

From 1964 to March 1972 all 'Discovering' books carried the imprint 'Shire Publications, Gubblecote Cross, Tring, Hertfordshire', or 'Shire Publications, Tring, Hertfordshire'. In May 1972 the partnership was merged with the magazine publishing company, which sold off its magazines and changed its name to Shire Publications Limited. All books subsequently carried the address '12B Temple Square, Aylesbury, Buckinghamshire' until the company moved to Cromwell House, Church Street, Princes Risborough, Buckinghamshire, in January 1974.

In April 1972 a second series of paperbacks, illustrated biographies called 'Lifelines', was launched. The series was devised by Richard Tames, who wrote the initial four: *Isambard Kingdom Brunel, General Gordon, William Morris* and *Josiah Wedgwood.* He wrote several more subsequently.

In May 1973 a third series, called Shire Albums, was started. The idea for these, and the texts of the first five titles, came from the country writer John Vince, author of several successful 'Discovering' books.

Subsequently, several new series were added to the list. In the first thirty years 840 titles were published.

How to read the entries

Entries in this bibliography take the following form: series number, title, author, year of publication, International Standard Book Number, number of pages, type of binding, details of the cover, quantity, subsequent editions. Fuller explanations are given below.

Series number. Most Shire books are published as part of a series and in most series each title is given a number, on the spine, the cover or the verso. The first books to be published by Shire – the 'Discovering' series – did not carry numbers until the publication of *Discovering Playing Cards and Tarots,* number 142 in the series. Numbers 1 to 141 were then allotted retrospectively to the previous titles in assumed order of publication. Subsequent printings of these earlier titles were numbered accordingly.

Title. Where the title of a book was changed in subsequent editions, this is given before the year of re-publication.

Author. Where an author's name or style was changed for subsequent editions, this appears before the year of re-publication.

Year of publication. Most titles published in the 1960s and 1970s also give the month of publication but this has been omitted from this bibliography.

Introduction

International Standard Book Number. ISBNs were not allotted until publication of *Discovering the Birmingham Road*, number 33 in the Discovering series. ISBNs were then allotted in retrospect to previous titles in the series, so they do not appear in the first editions of numbers 1 to 32. ISBNs are usually printed on the verso (page 2) but early titles had them on the title page and occasionally on page 3.

Number of pages. 'Discovering' books number the plate sections in with the text pages.

Type of binding. Shire books are paperbacked. 'Stitched' means saddle-stitched on the fold with two wires. 'Spined' titles have the board cover glued on to the pages to form a square back. Some early Shire books have broken up as the glue has become brittle. During 1972 and 1973 many titles broke up within five months of publication and were withdrawn for scrapping or rebinding. The 'Lifelines' series was particularly affected by this. Cased or hardbacked versions of three 'Discovering' books, numbers 22, 100 and 101, and two other titles, Shire Archaeology number 1 and History in Camera number 1, have been published. Four titles were published in hardback only: *The Complete Zodiac Entertainer*, *The Vampyre*, *The Early Barrow Diggers* and *From Antiquary to Archaeologist* (see under 'Non-series titles').

Cover. The subject matter of the cover design is given, as well as the name of the artist or designer and, in the case of line printed covers, the colours used in approximate order of predominance. The abbreviation ld means 'line drawing'; cp means 'colour photograph'.

Quantity . For first editions now out of print a quantity is given. This approximates to numbers printed and known to have been sold or circulated. Stocks that were withdrawn and scrapped have not been included in the quantity.

Subsequent editions. All editions are listed to date with year of publication and details of any non-textual changes from the previous edition. New impressions (reprints) have not been listed unless they have a bearing on the assembly of a collection.

Discovering INN SIGNS
Cadbury Lamb and Gordon Wright
Discovering CIVIC HERALDRY
Discovering CASTLES in central England
John Kinross
Discovering HORSE BRASSES
John Vince
Jack Gould
Discovering ABBEYS & PRIORIES
Geoffrey N. Wright
Discovering BRASSES
Malcolm Cook
Discovering THE BATH ROAD
Discovering ARCHAEOLOGY in England and Wales
James Dyer
Discovering SURNAMES
Their origins and meanings
J. W. Freeman
Discovering STATUES
J. D. Bennett
Discovering CROSSES
Christmas Customs and Folklore
A 'Discovering' guide to seasonal rites
Margaret Baker
Discovering TRACTION ENGINES
Harold Bonnett
Discovering CANALS
Leon Metcalfe and John Vince
Discovering Stained Glass
John Harries
Discovering BATTLEFIELDS in Northern England and Scotland
John Kinross
Discovering Coins
George Berry
Zoos, Bird Gardens & Animal Collections
Discovering HILL FIGURES
Kate Bergamar
Discovering Wayside Graves and Memorial Stones
Mark Chetwynd-Stapylton
Discovering WALL PAINTINGS
E. Clive Rouse
Discovering the Thames
Leon Metcalfe
Discovering Bells and Bellringing
Discovering ENGLISH FAIRS
Margaret Baker
Discovering TOPIARY
Margaret Baker
Discovering the EXETER ROAD
THIS OLD HOUSE
David Iredale
Discovering ENGLISH GARDENS

'DISCOVERING' BOOKS

'Discovering' books are non-fiction paperbacks, 177 mm by 113 mm, of varying length and either stitched or square-backed with spine. Most are printed on book wove paper and any section of black and white halftone illustrations (usually 8 or 16 pages) is printed on art paper. These are numbered in with the pages of the text.

1. *Discovering East Suffolk* (no author given), 1962, 24pp, stitched; cover: ld windmill by Stuart Herriott-Smith, grey and green. 10,000 copies. 2nd ed, 1963, author John Rotheroe on title page, 32pp; cover: grey and red, 'With a foreword by Simon Dewes'. 3rd ed, 1964, 36pp; cover: grey and blue. 4th ed, 1965, 36pp; cover: grey and red. 5th ed, 1967, 0 85263 049 2, 32pp; new cover: ld bridge scene, blue and tan. 6th ed, 1969, 32pp; cover: blue and purple.

2. *Discovering Norfolk* (no author given), 1965, 36pp, stitched; cover: ld windmill by Stuart Herriott-Smith, grey and red. 5000 copies. 2nd ed, 1968, 0 85263 057 3, author Cadbury Lamb, 32pp; cover: yellow and blue. 3rd ed, 1972, 0 85263 136 7, 40pp; new cover: cartouche above engraving of Norwich Cathedral, yellow and black. (The verso of this and subsequent printings incorrectly gives the first edition date as 1968.) 4th ed, 1976, 0 85263 352 1.

3. *Discovering Ipswich* (no author given), 1964, 28pp, stitched; cover: ld St Lawrence's, Ipswich, brown and blue. Hand printed and finished. 500 copies. (These have last page and back cover blank.) Reprinted 1965, 1500 copies. Although this was the second 'Discovering' book published, when the series numbers were allotted in 1972, it was mistakenly listed as third, and the 3rd and 4th editions of *Discovering Norfolk* were given the number 2.

4. *Discovering Wiltshire* Liz Tresilian, 1967, 0 85263 063 8, 40pp, stitched; cover: ld farmhouse scene by author, brown and blue. 5000 copies. (This was the first Shire title printed by Maund and Irvine of Tring, who printed the majority of the books from 1967 to 1976.) *Discovering Wiltshire* R. L. P. and Dorothy M. Jowitt, 1973, 0 85263 191 X, 64pp, stitched; cover: cartouche above engraving of Wilton House, brown and black. (This is a completely different book from the 1967 title, although it was given the same number in the series.)

5. *Discovering Castle Combe* Liz Tresilian, 1967, 0 85263 044 1, 16pp, stitched; cover: ld pack bridge by author. 4000 copies. The first impression has no date on the title page. 8th impression, 1981; new cover: cp market cross by Barbara Swanson.

6. *Discovering Buckinghamshire* Cadbury Lamb, 1967, 0 85263 041 7, 56pp, stitched; cover: ld Pann Mill, High Wycombe, by Lorna Cassidy, green and red. 5000 copies. 1968, cover lettering reversed out of red panels.

7. *Discovering West Suffolk* John Rotheroe, 1967, 0 85263 062 X, 32pp, stitched; cover: ld farmhouse scene by Liz Tresilian, green and red. 5000 copies.

8. *Discovering the Chilterns* J. H. B. Peel, 1967, 0 85263 046 8, 32pp, stitched; cover: ld bridge scene, brown and blue. 5000 copies.

9. *Discovering Brasses* Malcolm Cook, 1967, 0 85263 040 9, 48pp, stitched; cover: Thomas Cheyne brass, black and red. 5000 copies. Thirteen subsequent impressions, some erroneously called editions. 1970, cover title changed to *Discovering Brasses and Brass Rubbing*. 1971, spined. 1976, 0 85263 355 6. The imprint on the title page of the first printing has the printer's name before the publisher. This was reversed for the second impression. Subsequent impressions state number and date.

10. *Discovering Battlefields in Southern England* John Kinross, 1968, 0 85263 037 5, 64pp, stitched; cover: ld Royal Standard at Edgehill by Stuart Tresilian, blue and red. 10,000 copies. 1970, spine.

11. *Discovering English Fairs* Margaret Baker, 1968, 0 85263 050 6, 56pp, stitched; cover: Bewick engravings, orange and blue. 9800 copies.

12. *Discovering Hill Figures* Kate Bergamar, 1968, 0 85263 053 0, 48pp, stitched; cover: four hill figures in green and red. 10,000 copies. 2nd ed, 1972, 0 85263 157 X, spined; new cover: six figures in green and brown. 3rd ed, 1986, 0 85263 798 5, new cover: cp Westbury Horse.

13. *Discovering Windmills* J.N.T. Vince, 1968, 0 85263 064 6, 48pp, stitched; cover: ld Headcorn and Heckington mills by author, orange and black. 10,000 copies. 2nd ed, 1969, 0 85263 071 9, 64pp, spined; new cover: windmill design by Felix Partridge, brown blue and black. 3rd ed, John Vince, 1973, 0 85263 224 X, 56pp, cover colours reversed. 4th ed, 1977, 0 85263 373 4, 56pp, cover colours blue, wine and black. 5th ed,1981, 0 85263 567 2, 64pp; new cover: cp Stevington Mill. 6th ed, 1984, 0 85263 688 1, 72pp; new cover: cp Skidby Mill. 7th ed, 1987, 0 85263 888 4.

14. *This Old House* David Iredale, 1968, 0 85263 065 4, 64pp, stitched; cover: engraving of town plan, orange and blue. 10,000 copies. *Discovering This Old House*, 1970, spined; new cover: ld 'composite' house by Felix Partridge. 2nd ed, *Discovering Your Old House*, 1977, 0 85263 402 1. 3rd ed, David Iredale and John Barrett, 1991, 0 7478 0143 6, 112 pp; cover colours chestnut, beige and black.

15. *The American Story in England* Eric Rayner, 1968, 0 85263 035 2, 48pp, stitched; cover: ld ship by Rosalie Bullock, red and black. 5000 copies. In 1975 4000 original copies were re-covered, new title *Discovering American Origins*, new cover design of stars and stripes on map of England by Ron Shaddock, red and blue.

16. *The Bucks Explorer* Kate Bergamar, 1968, 0 85263 042 5, 56pp, stitched; cover: photo Moule's 1836 map of Bucks, pink and blue. 7000 copies.

17. *Discovering Oxfordshire* Cadbury Lamb, 1968, 0 85263 058 1, 48pp, stitched; cover: ld Ibstone Manor Farm by Lorna Cassidy, olive, red and black. 7500 copies.

18. *Discovering M1* Margaret Baker, 1968, 0 85263 055 7, 32pp, stitched; cover: ld motorway sign, blue and black. 5000 copies.

19. *Discovering the Bath Road* Margaret Baker, 1968, 0 85263 036 0, 48pp, stitched; cover: engraving 'The Mail Coach' by Henderson, blue and red. 6500 copies.

20. *Discovering Berkshire* Cadbury Lamb, 1968, 0 85263 039 5, 48pp, stitched; cover: ld

downland and market crosses by Rosalie Bullock, purple and blue. 7500 copies.

21. *Discovering Mermaids and Sea Monsters* Jane Hutchins, 1968, 0 85263 056 5, 40pp, stitched; cover: ld mermaid by Liz Tresilian, green and purple. 5000 copies.

22. *Discovering Wall Paintings* E. Clive Rouse, 1968, 0 85263 061 1, 48pp, stitched; cover: ld St Christopher by Jane Nicholson, purple and orange. 7000 copies. 2nd ed, 1971, spined, cover lettering reversed out of orange. 1000 copies hardbacked with dust jacket, 0 85263 134 0. 3rd ed, 1980, 0 85263 509 5; new cover: watercolour King David, Longthorpe Tower, by the author. (See *Medieval Wall Paintings*, an extended edition, in Non-series Titles).

23. *Discovering Castles in Eastern England* John Kinross, 1968, 0 85263 045 X, 48pp, stitched; cover: ld castle by Rosalie Bullock, red and black. 10,000 copies.

24. *Discovering Dorset* Annan Dickson, 1968, 0 85263 048 4, 48pp, stitched; cover: cp bluebell wood by Robert Glover. 7500 copies. 2nd ed, 1972, 0 85263 160 X, 56pp; new cover: cartouche above engraving of St Aldhelm's Head, green and black.

25. *Discovering the Exeter Road* Margaret Baker, 1968, 0 85263 051 4, 56pp, stitched; cover: engraving 'The Mail Coach' by Henderson, brown and blue. 3500 copies.

26. *Discovering the Gloucester Road* Eric Rayner, 1968, 0 85263 052 2, 48pp, stitched; cover: engraving 'The Mail Coach' by Henderson, violet and red. 3500 copies.

27. *Discovering Inn Signs* Cadbury Lamb and Gordon Wright, 1968, 0 85263 054 9, 64pp, stitched; cover: ld inn sign by Rosalie Bullock, brown and purple. 9000 copies. Reprinted 1970.

28. *Discovering Surrey* Barrie St Clair McBride, 1968, 0 85263 060 3, 40pp, stitched; cover: cp bluebell wood by Robert Glover. 6500 copies.

29. *Discovering Bells and Bellringing* John Camp, 1968, 0 85263 038 7, 48pp, stitched; cover: ld bells and ropes, red and black. 9500 copies. 2nd ed, 1975, 0 85263 290 8, spined; new cover: bells design by Ron Shaddock, red and black. 3rd ed, 1988, 0 85263 913 9; new cover: oil painting 'The Ringers of Launcells' by Frederick Smallfield.

30. *Discovering Canals* Leon Metcalfe and John Vince, 1968, 0 85263 043 3, 48pp, stitched; cover: scraperboard Three Locks by Edward Stamp, green and red. 9600 copies. Revised

(2nd ed), 1970. Revised (3rd ed), 1975, 0 85263 317 3, spined; new cover: ld lock gates and narrow boat by Ron Shaddock, blue red and black. (*Discovering Canals in Britain*, no. 257, is a different book.)

31. *Discovering Statues in Southern England* Margaret Baker, 1968, 0 85263 059 X, 64pp, stitched; cover: silhouette of Copper Horse, black and purple. 5000 copies.

32. *Christmas Customs and Folklore* Margaret Baker, 1968, 0 85263 047 6, 48pp, stitched; cover: scraperboard design by Edward Stamp, green and red. 9400 copies. 2nd ed (verso states reprinted), 1972, 0 85263 173 1, 56pp, spined; new cover: engraving 'Pickwick at Mr Wardle's' by Phiz, red green and black. 1979, *Discovering Christmas Customs and Folklore*; new cover: Santa Claus by Thomas Nast, blue red yellow and black.

33. *Discovering the Birmingham Road* Jack Gould, 1968, 0 85263 000 X, 48pp, stitched; cover: engraving 'The Mail Coach' by Henderson, green and purple. 2000 copies.

34. *Discovering Chesham* Val Biro and Arnold Baines, 1968, 0 85263 001 8, 24pp, stitched; cover: ld St Mary's, Chesham, by Val Biro, olive and black. 4000 copies.

35. *Discovering Surnames* J. W. Freeman, 1968, 0 85263 007 7, 64pp, stitched; cover: typographic, red and grey. 7500 copies. 1970, spined. 2nd ed (index added), 1973, 72pp; new cover: ld cartoon figures by Ron Shaddock, green red and black.

36. *The Wines of Madeira* Robert A. Lewis, 1968, 0 85263 003 4, 40pp, stitched; cover: photo wine lodge, black and brown. 15,000 copies.

37. *Discovering Battlefields in Northern England and Scotland* John Kinross, 1968, 0 85263 004 2, 64pp, stitched; cover: ld Royal Standard at Edgehill by Stuart Tresilian, black and red. 10,000 copies.

38. *Discovering Hallmarks on English Silver* John Bly, 1968, 0 85263 002 6, 56pp, stitched; cover: ld hallmarks by Edward Stamp, grey and black. 10,000 copies. July 1969, spined. 2nd ed, 1974, 0 85263 287 8, 64pp. 3rd ed, 1978, 0 85263 436 6. 4th ed, 1979, 0 85263 475 7. 5th ed, 1981, 0 85263 578 8. 6th ed, 1983, 0 85263 657 1. 7th ed, 1986, 0 85263 796 9. (In 1969 and 1970 the covers of some copies were overprinted with the names of retailers who purchased bulk quantities.)

39. *Discovering Civic Heraldry* F. E. Evans, 1968, 0 85263 005 0, 56pp, stitched; cover: ld heraldic beasts by Edward Stamp, blue and black. 10,000 copies.

40. *Discovering Coins* George Berry, 1968, 0 85263 011 5, 56pp, stitched; cover: ld coins by Edward Stamp, brown and black. 10,000 copies. 1969, spined.

41. *Discovering Devon* David Uttley and Dianne Toogood, 1969, 0 85263 010 7, 56pp, stitched; cover: three scraperboard scenes by Edward Stamp, olive and blue. 7500 copies.

42. *Discovering London Statues and Monuments* Margaret Baker, 1968, 0 85263 008 5, 72pp, stitched; cover: silhouette Sir Henry Havelock, black and purple. 10,000 copies. 2nd ed, 1980, 0 85263 520 6, 64pp, spined; new cover: ld statues in omnibus by Ron Shaddock, red yellow and black.

'Discovering' books

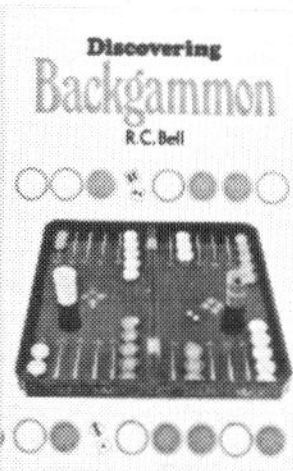

43. *Discovering Stained Glass* John Harries, 1968, 0 85263 006 9, 56pp, stitched; cover: ld angel by Edward Stamp, blue red and black. 7200 copies. 1970, spined. 2nd ed, 1980; new cover: cp St Thomas window.

44. *Discovering Horse Brasses* John Vince, 1968, 0 85263 014 X, 48pp, stitched; cover: ld horse brasses by Edward Stamp, brown and black. 10,000 copies. 1972, spined. 1985; new cover: cp six horse brasses.

45. *Discovering Warwickshire* George H. Haines, 1968, 0 85263 012 3, 48pp, stitched; cover: scraperboard Alcester by Edward Stamp, black and blue. 5000 copies.

46. *Discovering Archaeology in England and Wales* James Dyer, 1969, 0 85263 013 1, 80pp, stitched; cover: ld barrow excavation by M. Maitland Howard, green and brown. 10,000 copies. Revised, Dec 1969, spined. Revised (2nd ed), 1971. 3rd ed, 1973, 0 85263 241 X. 4th ed, 1976, 0 85263 340 8, 88pp. 1980; new cover: cp Pentre Ifan by E. A. Fulcher. 5th ed, 1985, 0 85263 705 5.

47. *Discovering the Thames* Leon Metcalfe, 1969, 0 85263 018 2, 56pp, stitched; cover: ld Arcadian figures by Edward Stamp, blue and green. 7600 copies. 2nd ed, 1981, 0 85263 566 4, spined; new cover: cp Thames cruisers by Derek Pratt.

48. *Discovering Wayside Graves and Memorial Stones* Mark Chetwynd- Stapylton, 1969, 0 85263 009 3, 40pp, stitched; cover: ld roadside gibbet by Edward Stamp, blue and black. 4800 copies.

49. *Discovering Statues in Central and Northern England* J. D. Bennett, 1969, 0 85263 016 6, 64pp, stitched; cover: silhouette Lady Godiva, black and purple. 3000 copies.

50. *Discovering Northamptonshire* Jack Gould, 1969, 0 85263 015 8, 64pp, stitched; cover: ld nine scenes by Edward Stamp, brown and black. 4200 copies. 1972; new cover: cartouche and engraving of riverside church, rose and black, remaining sheets from first printing bound into new covers. 2nd ed, 1977, 0 85263 341 6; new cover: cp Stoke Bruerne by Jeffery W. Whitelaw.

51. *Discovering Wargames* John Tunstill, 1969, 0 85263 021 2, 64pp, spined; cover: ld model cavalryman by Edward Stamp, red and black. 6800 copies. 1973; new cover: ld model officer and infantrymen by Ron Shaddock, olive blue and black.

52. *Discovering Topiary* Margaret Baker, 1969, 0 85263 019 0, 64pp, stitched; cover: ld peacock hedges by Edward Stamp, green and black. 4600 copies. 1975; new cover: similar design but price on back, remaining sheets from first printing bound into new covers.

53. *Discovering Castles in Central England* John Kinross, 1969, 0 85263 020 4, 56pp, stitched; cover: ld castle by Rosalie Bullock, brown and black. 7400 copies.

54. *Discovering Crosses* George H. Haines, 1969, 0 85263 022 0, 64pp, stitched; cover: ld crosses by Edward Stamp, grey and black. 7200 copies.

55. *Discovering Traction Engines* Harold Bonnett, 1969, 0 85263 024 7, 56pp, stitched; cover: ld Burrell engine by Edward Stamp, yellow and black. 7000 copies. 2nd ed, 1972, spined.

3rd ed, 1975, 0 85263 318 1. 4th ed, 1980, 0 85263 497 8; new cover: ld village scene by Ron Shaddock, brown blue green and black.

56. *Discovering English Gardens* Kay N. Sanecki, 1969, 0 85263 067 0, 80pp, spined; cover: ld landscape garden by Edward Stamp, green and black. 10,000 copies. *Discovering Gardens in Britain*, 1979, 0 85263 456 0; new cover: ld map of England by Ron Shaddock, blue green brown and black. 2nd ed, 1984, 0 85263 675 X; new cover: cp Hidcote Manor by Iris Hardwick. 3rd ed, 1987.

57. *Discovering Abbeys and Priories* Geoffrey N. Wright, 1969, 0 85263 068 9, 64pp, stitched; cover: ld Whitby Abbey by Edward Stamp, purple and black. 7100 copies. 1970, spined. 2nd ed, 1979, 0 85263 454 4; new cover: ld monks at work by Ron Shaddock, blue yellow red grey and black. 1985; new cover: cp Fountains Abbey.

58. *Discovering Gloucestershire* David and Dianne Uttley, 1969, 0 85263 017 4, 64pp, spined; cover: ld six scenes by Edward Stamp, brown and black. After 2500 copies sold, withdrawn because of errors. 1971, 62pp, plates reprinted and stock rebound in new cover: *Discovering Gloucestershire and the Cotswolds*, cartouche above engraving of Berkeley Castle, olive and black. 4400 copies.

59. *Discovering Hertfordshire* Margaret Baker, 1969, 0 85263 026 3, 56pp, stitched; cover: Bewick engravings, yellow and blue. 7500 copies. Reprinted.

60. *Discovering Hampshire* R. L. P. Jowitt, 1969, 0 85263 025 5, 56pp, stitched; cover: ld Selborne from The Hanger by Edward Stamp, green and black. 7200 copies. 2nd ed, *Discovering Hampshire and the New Forest* R. L. P. and Dorothy M. Jowitt, 1975, 0 85263 296 7; new cover: cartouche above engraving of Romsey Abbey, brown and black.

61. *Discovering Life-boats* E. W. Middleton, 1969, 0 85263 070 0, 80pp, spined; cover: ld lifeboat launch from beach by Edward Stamp, blue and black. 7000 copies. 2nd ed, 1972. 3rd ed, 1974.

62. *Discovering Lost Theatres* John Kennedy Melling, 1969, 0 85263 023 9, 72pp, spined; cover: ld toy theatre design by Robin Ollington, red and black. 4500 copies.

63. *Off-beat Walks in London* John Wittich and Ron Phillips, 1969, 0 85263 073 5, 64pp, spined; cover: ld Shakespeare and policeman by Felix Partridge, brown grey and black. 7300 copies. 2nd ed, 1973, 0 85263 227 4. 3rd ed, 1977, 0 85263 378 5. 4th ed, 1980, 0 85263 528 1. 5th ed, *Discovering Off-beat Walks in London*, 1990, 0 7478 0076 6.

64. *Discovering Saints in Britain* John Fidler, 1969, 0 85263 069 7, 72pp, spined; cover: ld two rows of saints by Rosalie Bullock, red blue and green. 9500 copies. 2nd ed, John Vince, 1979, 0 85263 449 8, 64pp; new cover: ld saints by Ron Shaddock, gold red and black. 1990; new cover: watercolours of saints by Rachel Lewis.

65. *Discovering Regional Archaeology: Eastern England* James Dyer, 1969, 0 85263 074 3, 72pp, spined; cover: ld Boudicca sacking Colchester by M. Maitland Howard, orange and black. 6200 copies. 2nd ed, 1973, 0 85263 228 2, cover change: ld on white panel.

66. *Discovering English Customs and Traditions* Margaret Gascoigne, 1969, 0 85263 072 7,

76pp, spined; cover: ld posters on wood-grained background by Robin Ollington, brown blue and black. 8500 copies. 2nd ed, 1980, 0 85263 506 0, 64pp; new cover: coloured print 'Chimney-sweeper on the first of May' *c*.1810.

67. *Discovering Military Traditions* Arthur Taylor, 1969, 0 85263 078 6, 68pp, spined; cover: ld drummer on parade by Edward Stamp, grey red and black. 8500 copies. 2nd ed, 1972, 0 85263 171 5, 72pp; new cover: ld Union Jack and Royal Artillery badge by Robin Ollington, black red and blue.

68. *Discovering London Railway Stations* John Camp, 1969, 0 85263 079 4, 56pp, spined; cover: ld engine and station by Robin Ollington, yellow brown and black. 7000 copies.

69. *Discovering Church Furniture* Christopher Howkins, 1969, 0 85263 075 1, 80pp, spined; cover: ld lectern and candelabra by Felix Partridge, brown purple and beige. 9200 copies. 2nd ed, 1980.

70. *Discovering Trade Tokens* George Berry, 1969, 0 85263 028 X, 56pp, spined; cover: ld shop scene and tokens by Felix Partridge, grey brown and black. 7200 copies.

71. *Discovering Folklore in Industry* Alan Smith, 1969, 0 85263 077 8, 48pp, stitched; cover: ld eight scenes by Edward Stamp, blue red and black. 4600 copies.

72. *Discovering Staffordshire Figures of the Nineteenth Century* Amoret and Christopher Scott, 1969, 0 85263 081 6, 68pp, spined; cover: ld Heenan and Sayers figures by Felix Partridge, red yellow and black. 9300 copies.

73. *Discovering Militaria* Peter Newman, 1969, 0 85263 076 X, 60pp, spined; cover: ld helmet and military items by Robin Ollington, red and black. 9000 copies. 2nd ed, 1972, 0 85263 144 8, 64pp.

74. *Discovering the Folklore of Plants* Margaret Baker, 1969, 0 85263 080 8, 72pp, spined; cover: ld mandrake by Felix Partridge, grey yellow and purple. 10,000 copies. 2nd ed, 1980, 0 85263 491 9, 64pp.

75. *Discovering Bridges* Leon Metcalfe, 1970, 0 85263 086 7, 56pp, spined; cover: ld bridge and skiff by Felix Partridge, yellow blue and brown. 7300 copies.

76. *Discovering British Postage Stamps* C. W. Hill, 1970, 0 85263 083 2, 72pp, spined; cover: ld stamp design by Felix Partridge, blue brown and black. 8800 copies.

77. *Discovering Towns* John Haddon, 1970, 0 85263 082 4, 92pp, spined; cover: ld tourists in townscape by Felix Partridge, blue red and grey. 7600 copies. 1977; remaining stock rebound in new cover: ld street frontages by Ron Shaddock, red ochre and black.

78. *Discovering High Wycombe* Lorna Cassidy, 1970, 0 85263 094 8, 24pp, stitched; cover: ld High Street by the author, brown and red. 3000 copies.

79. *Discovering Smoking Antiques* Amoret and Christopher Scott, 1970, 0 85263 085 9, 56pp, spined; cover: ld tobacco cabinet and pipe by Robin Ollington, blue brown and black. 5000 copies.

80. *Discovering Watermills* John Vince, 1970, 0 85263 087 5, 56pp, spined; cover: ld mill and reflection by Felix Partridge, green and black. 10,000 copies. 2nd ed, 1976, 0 85263 333 5. 3rd ed, 1980, 0 85263 510 9, 64pp; new cover: cp Harnham Mill. 4th ed, 1984, 0 85263 687 3, 80pp; new cover: cp Sturminster Newton Mill. 5th ed, 1987, 0 85263 887 6.

81. *Discovering Wrought Iron* G. J. Hollister-Short, 1970, 0 85263 084 0, 72pp, spined; cover: ld Tijou mask by Felix Partridge, green and black. 7300 copies.

82. *Discovering Leicestershire and Rutland* J. D. Bennett, 1970, 0 85263 092 1, 48pp, stitched; cover: engravings of obelisk and Lutterworth church, orange and black. 5000 copies. 2nd ed, 1973, 0 85263 190 1, 56pp; new cover: cartouche above engraving of Lutterworth church, orange and black.

83. *Discovering English County Regiments* Arthur Taylor, 1970, 0 85263 095 6, 64pp, spined; cover: ld ram mascot of Sherwood Foresters by the author, yellow red and blue. 9700 copies. 2nd ed, 1987, 0 85263 708 X, 56pp; new cover: painting 'The 14th Foot at Waikato Paa, New Zealand, 1863' by Orlando Norie.

84. *Discovering Flower Arrangement* Betty Massingham, 1970, 0 85263 088 3, 64pp, spined; cover: ld hand with rose by Felix Partridge, black yellow and pink. 9000 copies.

85. *Discovering Schools* George Berry, 1970, 0 85263 091 3, 80pp, spined; cover: line and wash masters and pupils by Felix Partridge, yellow purple and brown. 7300 copies.

86. *Discovering England's Trees* Miles Hadfield, 1970, 0 85263 089 1, 92pp, spined; cover: ld tree trunk by Felix Partridge, brown blue and yellow. 9000 copies. 2nd ed, 1980, 0 85263 490 0, 96pp; new cover: cp Claremont landscape and lake.

87. *Discovering Carts and Wagons* John Vince, 1970, 0 85263 097 2, 56pp, spined; cover: ld wagon in roundel by David Wray, blue red and black. 10,000 copies. 2nd ed, 1974, 0 85263 284 3. 3rd ed, 1987, 0 85263 885 X, 72pp; new cover: mezzotint of Morland scene with cart.

88. *Discovering Yorkshire: the Moors and the Coast* Arthur Gaunt, 1970, 0 85263 098 0, 56pp, stitched; cover: engraving of Castle Howard, green and black. 7300 copies.

89. *Discovering Herbs* Kay N. Sanecki, 1970, 0 85263 100 6, 56pp, spined; cover: ld herbs in paving, blue and green. 10,000 copies. 2nd ed, 1973; cover change, yellow blue and black. 3rd ed, 1982, 0 85263 586 9, 64pp; new cover: cp herb garden at Castle Drogo. 4th ed, 1985, 0 85263 719 5.

90. *Discovering Model Soldiers* Arthur Taylor, 1970, 0 85263 099 9, 48pp, stitched; cover: ld four model figures by the author, yellow red and black. 10,000 copies. 2nd ed, 1972, 0 85263 172 3, 60pp, spined; cover: ld three model figures by Robin Ollington, green orange and black.

91. *Discovering Regional Archaeology: Central England* Barry M. Marsden, 1970, 0 85263 096 4, 64pp, spined; cover: scraperboard, massacre at Sutton Walls by M. Maitland Howard, brown and black. 7000 copies.

92. *Discovering Picture Postcards* C. W. Hill, 1970, 0 85263 102 2, 64pp, spined; cover: ld

postcards by Robin Ollington, blue red and black. 10,000 copies. 2nd ed, 1978, 0 85263 411 0; new cover: ld comic husband and wife by Ron Shaddock, blue red and black.

93. *Your Family Tree* David Iredale, 1970, 0 85263 104 9, 64pp, spined; cover: manuscript family tree, yellow red and black. 10,000 copies. 2nd ed, *Discovering Your Family Tree*, 1973, 0 85263 193 6, 72pp; new cover: ld figures in a family tree by Ron Shaddock, blue red and black. 3rd ed, 1977, 0 85263 404 8, 64pp. 4th ed, David Iredale and John Barrett, 1985, 0 85263 767 5, 72pp.

94. *Discovering Highwaymen* Russell Ash, 1970, 0 85263 101 4, 48pp, stitched; cover: ld highwayman by Edward Stamp, black and red. 7500 copies.

95. *Discovering Regional Archaeology: The Cotswolds and the Upper Thames* James Dyer, 1970, 0 85263 107 3, 56pp, spined; cover: scraperboard Whispering Knights legend by M. Maitland Howard, green and black. 9900 copies.

96. *Discovering Regional Archaeology: South-western England* Leslie Grinsell, 1970, 0 85263 106 5, 64pp, spined; cover: ld quoit burial chamber by M. Maitland Howard, blue and black. 9600 copies.

97. *Discovering Antique Firearms* Dennis Lack, 1971, 0 85263 108 1, 64pp, spined; cover: ld flintlock pistol, green and black. 10,300 copies.

98. *Discovering Antique Maps* A. G. Hodgkiss, 1971, 0 85263 111 1, 72pp, spined; cover: two cartouches on map of Bucks, red cream and black. 10,000 copies. 2nd ed, 1975, 0 85263 289 4. 3rd ed, 1977, 0 85263 389 0. 4th ed, 1981, 0 85263 581 8; new cover: cp single cartouche on Saxton's map of Dorset.

99. *Discovering Embroidery of the Nineteenth Century* Santina Levey, 1971, 0 85263 113 8, 64pp, spined; cover: ld William Morris flower pot design by Robin Ollington, blue pink and green. 9500 copies. 2nd ed, 1977, 0 85263 398 X. 1983, new cover: cp Berlin woolwork panel with cockatoo.

100. *Discovering English Furniture 1500-1720* John Bly, 1971, 0 85263 109 X, 64pp, spined; cover: ld chair in mirror by Robin Ollington, green gold and black. 13,800 copies. A further 1000 copies hardbacked with dust jacket, 0 85263 132 4.

101. *Discovering English Furniture 1720-1830* John Bly, 1971, 0 85263 110 3, 72pp, spined; cover: ld chair in mirror by Robin Ollington, maroon gold and black. 16,000 copies. A further 1000 copies hardbacked with dust jacket, 0 85263 133 2.

102. *Discovering Place-names* John Field, 1971, 0 85263 112 X, 56pp, spined; cover: typographic, green and grey. 9500 copies. 2nd ed, 1976, 0 85263 356 4; new cover: ld map of British Isles by Ron Shaddock, blue beige and black. 3rd ed, 1984, 0 85263 702 0, 72pp.

103. *Discovering Burford* Sarah E. Wise, 1971, 0 85263 120 0, 24pp, stitched; cover: photo Tolsey, red and black. 2800 copies.

104. *Discovering Cheshire* Joan P. Alcock, 1971, 0 85263 117 0, 56pp, stitched; cover: cartouche above engraving of Rows in Chester. 7000 copies. 2nd ed, 1975, 0 85263 297 5.

105. *Discovering Essex* S. M. Jarvis, 1971, 0 85263 124 3, 68pp, stitched; cover: cartouche above engraving of St Botolph's Priory. 9500 copies. 2nd ed, 1977, 0 85263 370 X; new cover: cartouche above cp Wivenhoe by Jeffery W. Whitelaw.

106. *Discovering Sea Shells* Barry Charles, 1971, 0 85263 090 5, 56pp, spined; cover: ld shells by Edwin Patterson, blue yellow and black. 8300 copies.

107. *Discovering Spas* R. L. P. and Dorothy M. Jowitt, 1971, 0 85263 119 7, 64pp, spined; cover: ld spa scene with rotunda by Edward Stamp, blue green and black. 3000 copies.

108. *Discovering Windsor* David and Beryl Hedges, 1971, 0 85263 123 5, 56pp, stitched; cover: ld round tower and sentry by Robin Ollington, blue red and black. 7500 copies.

109. *Discovering Lincolnshire* David Kaye, 1971, 0 85263 116 2, 64pp, stitched; cover: cartouche above engraving of triangular bridge at Croyland, pink and black. 7500 copies. 2nd ed, 1976, 0 85263 308 4; new cover: cartouche above engraving of Boston Stump, olive and black.

110. *Discovering London for Children* Margaret M. Pearson, 1971, 0 85263 121 9, 96pp, spined; cover: ld dinosaur and yeoman warder by Felix Partridge, red yellow and black. 11,000 copies. 2nd ed, 1972. 3rd ed, 1976, 0 85263 310 6. 4th ed, 1978, 0 85263 429 3, 88pp. 5th ed, 1980, 0 85263 521 4, 80pp. 6th ed, 1983, 0 85263 628 8, 96pp. 7th ed, 1985, 0 85263 709 8, 104pp. 8th ed, 1987, 0 85263 889 2.

111. *Discovering Regional Archaeology: Wessex* Leslie Grinsell and James Dyer, 1971, 0 85263 122 7, 80pp, spined; cover: engraving Stonehenge, brown and black. 10,000 copies.

112. *Discovering Cathedrals* David Pepin, 1971, 0 85263 125 1, 80 pp, spined; cover: ld Ely Cathedral by the author, blue grey and black. 12,200 copies. 2nd ed, 1974, 0 85263 279 7. 3rd ed, 1977, 0 85263 374 2; new cover: ld Lincoln Cathedral by Ron Shaddock, blue brown and black. 4th ed, 1979, 0 85263 472 2; new cover: ld Worcester Cathedral by Ron Shaddock, green blue brown and black. 5th ed, 1985, 0 85263 718 7; new cover: cp Rochester Cathedral.

113. *Discovering Regional Archaeology: North Eastern England* Barry M. Marsden, 1971, 0 85263 115 4, 64pp, spined; cover: scraperboard hunter and stag by M. Maitland Howard, purple and black. 7000 copies.

114. *Discovering Regional Archaeology: North Western England* Barry M. Marsden, 1971, 0 85263 114 6, 56pp, spined; cover: scraperboard Hadrian's Wall by M. Maitland Howard, blue and black. 7300 copies.

115. *Discovering the Folklore of Birds and Beasts* Venetia Newall, 1971, 0 85263 126 X, 72pp, spined; cover: Bewick owl and bull, pink and black. 9800 copies.

116. *Discovering Toys and Toy Museums* Pauline Flick, 1971, 0 85263 118 9, 64pp, spined; cover: ld dolls' house by Liz Tresilian, pink purple and orange. 6800 copies. 2nd ed, 1977, 0 85263 391 2, 72pp; new cover: ld rocking horse and other toys by Ron Shaddock, pink purple and orange.

new cover: cp kittiwake and chick by the author.

156. *Discovering Christian Names* S. M. Jarvis, 1973, 0 85263 189 8, 64pp, spined; cover: ld family group by Mike Smith, violet green and black. 14,500 copies. 2nd ed, 1979, 0 85263 448 X; new cover: ld four panels of cartoon figures by Ron Shaddock, brown beige and black.

157. *Discovering British Cavalry Regiments* Arthur Taylor, 1973, 0 85263 192 8, 72pp, spined; cover: ld cavalry group by Malcolm Greensmith, red gold and black. 9200 copies.

158. *Discovering Local History* David Iredale, 1973, 0 85263 194 4, 72pp, spined; cover: printed ephemera, black and brown. 9800 copies. 2nd ed, 1977, 64pp; new cover: ld town plan with cartoon figures by Ron Shaddock, brown yellow and black. 1985; cover change: yellow omitted.

159. *Discovering the Thames and Chilterns* The Thames and Chilterns Tourist Board, 1974, 0 85263 153 7, 80pp, stitched; cover: pen and wash Windsor Castle by Brian Elliott, blue red and black. 18,700 copies. 2nd ed, 1976, 0 85263 301 7, spined; new cover: ld Christ Church, Oxford, by Ron Shaddock, green blue red and black.

160. *Discovering Old Motor Cycles* T. E. Crowley, 1973, 0 85263 195 2, 56pp, spined; cover: photo of 1906 Touring Quadrant, design by Robin Ollington, green brown and black. 9700 copies. 2nd ed, 1977, 0 85263 390 4. 3rd ed, 1981, 0 85263 557 5. 4th ed, 1984, 0 85263 703 9.

161. *Discovering Famous Battles: Marlborough's Campaigns* I. F. W. Beckett, 1973, 0 85263 196 0, 64pp, spined; cover: Malplaquet, design by Robin Ollington, green red and black. 7300 copies.

162. *Discovering Famous Battles: The Peninsular War* R. J. Wilkinson-Latham, 1973, 0 85263 197 9, 80pp, spined; cover: design by Robin Ollington, violet red and black. 7400 copies.

163. *Discovering English Civil Wargaming* ed. John Tunstill, 1973, 0 85263 198 7, 48pp, spined; cover: ld Battle of Holman's Bridge by Stuart Tresilian, blue brown and black. 5600 copies.

164. *Discovering Stately Homes* Amoret and Christopher Scott, 1973, 0 85263 211 8, 88pp, spined; cover: ld armour and houses by Robin Ollington, green blue and black. 9800 copies. 2nd ed, 1975, 0 85263 303 3. 3rd ed, 1981, 0 85263 554 0, 96pp; new cover: cp Wimpole Hall. 4th ed, 1989, 0 85263 993 7.

165. *Discovering London Curiosities* John Wittich, 1973, 0 85263 212 6, 76pp, spined; cover: ld Achilles statue by Felix Partridge, brown pink and black. 9300 copies. 2nd ed, 1980, 0 85263 507 9, 64pp. 3rd ed, 1990, 0 7478 0074 X; new cover: print 'A New Love Song' from 'Cries of London' by F. Wheatley.

166. *Discovering Wild Plant Names* John E. Stevens, 1973, 0 85263 213 4, 64pp, spined; cover: ld flowers by Molly Hyde, design by Ron Shaddock, green yellow and black. 9700 copies. Reprinted.

167. *Discovering English Literary Associations* Sidney Blackmore, 1973, 0 85263 214 2, 80pp, spined; cover: five portrait engravings, green red and black. 9500 copies.

168. *Discovering Orienteering* Tony Walker, 1973, 0 85263 215 0, 48pp, spined; cover: ld control marker and map by Mike Smith, red brown and black. 7500 copies. 2nd ed, *Discovering Orienteering and Wayfaring*, 1979, 0 85263 468 4; cover change: redesigned with new title.

169. *Discovering Monuments* J. D. Bennett, 1973, 0 85263 216 9, 64pp, spined; cover: ld Forbury Lion, Reading, by Mike Smith, green blue yellow and black. 2600 copies.

170. *Discovering Walks in Hertfordshire* Ron Pigram, 1973, 0 85263 217 7, 56pp, spined; cover: ld stile and village in oval by Edward Stamp, blue brown yellow and black. 7300 copies. 2nd ed, 1985, 0 85263 742 X; new cover: cp Ashwell.

171. *Discovering Lancashire* Joan P. Alcock, 1977, 0 85263 218 5, 56pp, stitched; cover: cp Tarnbrook Wyre by Michael Edwards. 4800 copies. The original series number and ISBN were kept despite delays in publication.

172. *Discovering Walks in Oxford and Cambridge* Keith Baverstock, 1973, 0 85263 219 3, 68pp, spined; cover: ld arches and street scene by Felix Partridge, brown orange and black. 3200 copies.

173. *Discovering Walks in Edinburgh* Keith and Fiona Baverstock, 1973, 0 85263 220 7, 48pp, stitched; cover: ld townscape by Felix Partridge, blue yellow and crimson. 5200 copies.

174. *Discovering Battlefields of Scotland* John Kinross, 1976, 0 85263 221 5, 48pp, spined; cover: ld knights in battle by Ron Shaddock, blues and black. 5200 copies. The original series number and ISBN were kept despite delays in publication. 2nd ed, *Discovering Scottish Battlefields*, 1985, 0 85263 750 0; new cover: lithograph 'The Field of Preston Pans'.

175. *Discovering Staffordshire* Joan P. Alcock, 1973, 0 85263 222 3, 56pp, stitched; cover: cartouche above engraving of Tamworth Castle, violet and black. 7300 copies.

176. *Discovering Battlefields of England* John Kinross, 1973, 0 85263 223 1, 136pp, spined; cover: ld knights in battle by Ron Shaddock, greens and black. The texts of *Discovering Battlefields in Southern England* and *Discovering Battlefields in Northern England and Scotland* revised and part combined in this one volume. 7700 copies. 2nd ed, 1979, 0 85263 447 1, 128pp. 3rd ed, 1989, 144pp; new cover: cp Richard III's standard at Bosworth Battlefield.

177. *Discovering Pantomime* Gyles Brandreth, 1973, 0 85263 230 4, 56pp, spined; cover: ld dame by Ron Shaddock, yellow blue and black. 7500 copies.

178. *Discovering Lost Railways* F. G. Cockman, 1973, 0 85263 231 2, 88pp, spined; cover: ld rusting steam locomotives by Felix Partridge, brown green and black. 9500 copies. 2nd ed, 1976, 0 85263 325 4. 3rd ed, 1980, 0 85263 492 7. 4th ed, 1985, 0 85263 722 5; new cover: cp Braunston and Willoughby station by the author. 5th ed, 1988, 0 85263 916 3.

179. *Discovering Mottoes, Slogans and War Cries* Douglas Taylor, 1973, 0 85263 232 0, 64pp, spined; cover: ld knight with banner by Ron Shaddock, brown and black. 4700 copies.

142. *Discovering Playing Cards and Tarots* George Beal, 1972, 0 85263 166 9, 56pp, spined; cover: ld double-ended king by Robin Ollington, gold red and black. 6900 copies. The first Discovering title to bear its number in the series.

143. *Investing Your Money* Gordon Wells, 1972, 0 85263 167 7, 56pp, spined; cover: ld bemused investor by Mike Smith, red green and black. 3700 copies.

144. *Discovering Epitaphs* Geoffrey N. Wright, 1972, 0 85263 170 7, 64pp, spined; cover: ld gravestone by Robin Ollington, grey and green. 7000 copies. Reprinted.

145. *Discovering Oil Lamps* Cecil A. Meadows, 1972, 0 85263 168 5, 48pp, spined; cover: engravings of lamps, design by Robin Ollington, green maroon and black. 7200 copies. 2nd ed, 1974, 0 85263 288 6.

146. *Discovering Banknotes* Kenneth Lake, 1972, 0 85263 165 0, 56pp, spined; cover: banknotes design by Antony Wheeler, blue green and black. 5600 copies.

147. *Discovering Ghosts* Leon Metcalfe, 1972, 0 85263 169 3, 64pp, spined; cover: ld headless coachman by Felix Partridge, red grey and black. 7500 copies. Reprinted.

148. *Discovering British Military Badges and Buttons* R. J. Wilkinson-Latham, 1973, 0 85263 178 2, 80pp, spined; cover: ld badges and buttons by Edward Stamp, red gold and black. 9800 copies. 1986; new cover: cp East Surrey Regiment helmet by Stephen Fitzjohn.

149. *Discovering Modelling for Wargamers* Dennis C. Teague, 1973, 0 85263 181 2, 48pp, spined; cover: photo model cavalryman and Waterloo map, design by Malcolm Greensmith, yellow red and black. 8400 copies.

150. *Discovering Victorian and Edwardian Furniture* John Bly, 1973, 0 85263 182 0, 72pp, spined; cover: ld chair in mirror by Robin Ollington, blue gold and black. 10,000 copies.

151. *Discovering Kings and Queens* D. E. Wickham, 1973, 0 85263 179 0, 88pp, spined; cover: ld Henry VIII and wives by Felix Partridge, blue pink and black. 9800 copies. 2nd ed, 1976, 0 85263 309 2; new cover: ld Victoria, Henry VII, Mary and James I by Ron Shaddock, purple and black. 3rd ed, 1978, 0 85263 439 0. 1983; new cover: oil painting 'The Happier Days of Charles I' by Frederick Goodall.

152. *Discovering Castles in England and Wales* John Kinross, 1973, 0 85263 183 9, 280pp, spined; cover: ld knight and castle by Malcolm Greensmith, blue brown and black. 19,000 copies. 2nd ed, 1984, 0 85263 686 5, 176pp; new cover: cp Orford Castle.

153. *Discovering Somerset* David and Dianne Uttley, 1973, 0 85263 180 4, 64pp, stitched; cover: cartouche above engraving of Glastonbury Abbey, blue and black. 6900 copies.

154. *Discovering Ecology* Patrick H. Armstrong, 1973, 0 85263 184 7, 72pp, spined; cover: ld hedgerow animals by Edward Stamp, brown yellow blue and black. 10,000 copies. 2nd ed, 1979, 0 85263 413 7.

155. *Discovering Bird Watching* Jim Flegg, 1973, 0 85263 185 5, 96pp, spined; cover: ld bird watcher and cliffs by Mike Smith, crimson blue and black. 19,500 copies. 2nd ed, 1984;

'Discovering' books

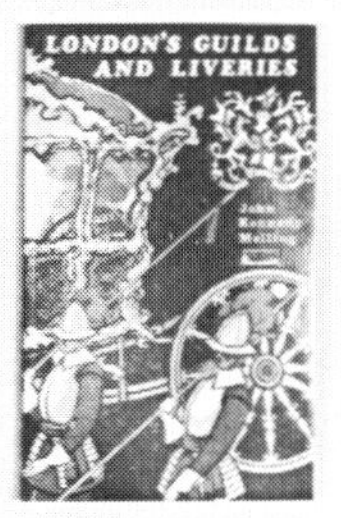

117. *Discovering Comics* Denis Gifford, 1971, 0 85263 128 6, 64pp, spined; cover: ld panels of comic characters by the author, blue orange and black. 6800 copies. 2nd ed, 1991, 0 7478 0108 8, 72pp; new cover: cp *Happy Days* comic by Roy Wilson.

118. *Rules for Wargaming* Arthur Taylor, 1971, 0 85263 127 8, 68pp, spined; cover: ld Napoleonic battle by Stuart Tresilian, design by Mike Smith, green red and black. 7500 copies. 2nd ed, 1972.

119. *Discovering Harness and Saddlery* G. Tylden, 1971, 0 85263 105 7, 56pp, spined; cover: ld horse's head and saddlery by Edward Stamp, blue brown and black. 6800 copies. Reprinted.

120. *Discovering Railwayana* Donald J. Smith, 1971, 0 85263 129 4, 64pp, spined; cover: ld railway lamps and signs by Robin Ollington, blue brown and black. 9800 copies.

121. *Discovering Ship Models* Norman Boyd, 1971, 0 85263 130 8, 56pp, spined; cover: ld nef by Felix Partridge, green blue and black. 7500 copies.

122. *Discovering British Military Uniforms* Arthur Taylor, 1972, 0 85263 131 6, 80pp, spined; cover: ld dragoon shako, hussar and lancer by the author, design by Mike Smith, orange blue and black. 12,000 copies. 1987; new cover: cp 'The Hampshire Regiment' by R. Simpkin.

123. *Discovering Artillery* R. J. Wilkinson-Latham, 1972, 0 85263 135 9, 72pp, spined; cover: ld carronade and field guns by Mike Smith, purple red and black. 7600 copies. 2nd ed, 1987, 0 85263 707 1; new cover: cp 'Peace Manoeuvres: A Field Battery, Royal Artillery' by R. Simpkin.

124. *Discovering Edged Weapons* John Wilkinson-Latham, 1972, 0 85263 138 3, 64pp, spined; cover: ld crossed swords by Robin Ollington, gold red and black. 9400 copies.

125. *Discovering Suffolk* John Rotheroe, 1972, 0 85263 137 5, 64pp, stitched; cover: cartouche above engraving of Burgh Castle, blue and black. The texts of *Discovering East Suffolk* and *Discovering West Suffolk* revised and combined in one volume. 7300 copies. Revised (2nd ed), 1973. 3rd ed, 1975, 0 85263 302 5; cover change: cartouche above engraving of Norman tower at Bury St Edmunds. 4th ed, 1977, 0 85263 372 6; new cover: cp Cavendish by Jeffery W. Whitelaw.

126. *Discovering Space* Ian Ridpath, 1972, 0 85263 139 1, 64pp, spined; cover: ld Apollo lunar module by Felix Partridge, blue and black. 5000 copies. 1978, remaining stock rebound in new cover: *Discovering Space and Astronomy*, photo moon by Ron Shaddock, black cream and blue.

127. *Discovering Forests of Central England* Jack Gould, 1972, 0 85263 149 9, 64pp, spined; cover: ld fallow deer by Edward Stamp, brown blue and black. 4100 copies.

128. *Gardening for the Handicapped* Betty Massingham, 1972, 0 85263 145 6, 60pp, spined; cover: ld urn and cartouche by Robin Ollington, blue yellow and black. 7500 copies.

129. *Discovering Period Gardens* John Anthony, 1972, 0 85263 146 4, 72pp, spined; cover: ld

fountain by Liz Tresilian, green blue and brown. 7500 copies. 2nd ed, 1985, 0 85263 724 1; new cover: cp Westbury Court.

130. *Discovering Sussex* R. L. P. Jowitt, 1972, 0 85263 148 0, 72pp, stitched; cover: cartouche above engraving of Pevensey Bay, turquoise and black. 7200 copies. R. L. P. and Dorothy M. Jowitt, 1973. 2nd ed, 1976, 0 85263 363 7.

131. *Discovering Worcestershire and Herefordshire* Walter Stranz, 1972, 0 85263 147 2, 64pp, stitched; cover: cartouche above engraving of Evesham parish churches, red and black. 7300 copies.

132. *Discovering Caves* Tony and Anne Oldham, 1972, 0 85263 155 3, 52pp, spined; cover: ld show cave by Mike Smith, black blue and green. 7600 copies.

133. *Footsteps through London's Past* Keith Baverstock, 1972, 0 85263 150 2, 56pp, spined; cover: ld Sherlock Holmes by Felix Partridge, grey black and crimson. 9600 copies.

134. *Discovering Narrow Gauge Railways* James Buck, 1972, 0 85263 152 9, 80pp, spined; cover: ld engine 'P. C. Allen' by Alfred R. Fisher, purple black and orange. 9400 copies.

135. *Discovering Old Buses and Trolley Buses* David Kaye, 1972, 0 85263 154 5, 60pp, spined; cover: ld 1912 Tilling-Stevens bus by Robin Ollington, green yellow and brown. 9200 copies.

136. *Discovering Walks in the Chilterns* Ron Pigram, 1972, 0 85263 151 0, 60pp, spined; cover: ld stile and village in oval by Edward Stamp, brown blue yellow and black. 7500 copies. 2nd ed, 1982, 0 85263 615 6, 64pp; new cover: cp Nettleden. 3rd ed, 1989, 0 85263 991 0.

137. *Discovering Churches* John Harries, 1972, 0 85263 156 1, 104pp, spined; cover: ld church and lych-gate by Dennis Lack, blue brown and black. 18,000 copies. 2nd ed, 1979, 0 85263 471 4. 1984; new cover: watercolour church and cattle by Thomas Barker.

138. *Discovering Yorkshire: West Riding* Frank Beckwith jnr, 1972, 0 85263 162 6, 60pp, stitched; cover: cartouche above engraving of Wakefield bridge chapel, brown and black. 6900 copies.

139. *Discovering the Westward Stage* Margaret Baker, Jack Gould and Eric Rayner, 1972, 0 85263 164 2, 200pp, spined; cover: ld finger post and coach by Robin Ollington, yellow blue and black. 2500 copies. Comprises the text pages of *Discovering the Bath Road, Discovering the Birmingham Road, Discovering the Exeter Road* and *Discovering the Gloucester Road* with new title page and verso.

140. *Discovering Derbyshire and the Peak District* Joan P. Alcock, 1972, 0 85263 161 8, 68pp, stitched; cover: cartouche above engraving of lead mine, grey and black. 7300 copies. 2nd ed, 1976, 0 85263 362 9.

141. *Discovering Archaeology in Denmark* James Dyer, 1972, 0 85263 158 8, 88pp, spined; cover: photo Tollund Man and burial chamber, design by Robin Ollington, blue green and black. 2600 copies.

180. *Discovering London's Guilds and Liveries* John Kennedy Melling, 1973, 0 85263 233 9, 88pp, spined; cover: ld Lord Mayor's coach by Felix Partridge, yellow red green and black. 'Discovering' omitted. 7000 copies. 2nd ed, 1978, 0 85263 442 0; cover change: full title relettered. 3rd ed, 1981, 0 85263 553 2, 80pp. 4th ed, 1988, 0 85263 971 6; new cover: oil painting of Westminster Bridge and guild barge, *c*.1750.

181. *Discovering Old Bicycles* T. E. Crowley, 1973, 0 85263 234 7, 56pp, spined; cover: photo 'penny farthing' and rider, design by Robin Ollington, green brown and black. 7200 copies. 2nd ed, 1978, 0 85263 437 4.

182. *Discovering Old Board Games* R. C. Bell, 1973, 0 85263 235 5, 80pp, spined; cover: board design by Ron Shaddock, red yellow and black. 9000 copies. 2nd ed, 1980, 0 85263 533 8; new cover: photo Tablan board and throwing sticks, brown and black.

183. *Discovering Regional Archaeology: South Eastern England* Edward Sammes, 1973, 0 85263 240 1, 80pp, spined; cover: engraving Portchester Castle, rose and black. 7200 copies.

184. *Discovering Regional Archaeology: Wales* Ilid Anthony, 1973, 0 85263 163 4, 80pp, spined; cover: engraving Bryn-Celli-Ddu chambered tomb, green and black. 5000 copies.

185. *Discovering Theatre Ephemera* John Kennedy Melling, 1974, 0 85263 245 2, 56pp, spined; cover: play bill and ephemera by Robin Ollington, brown red and black. 5000 copies.

186. *Discovering French and German Military Uniforms* Arthur Taylor, 1974, 0 85263 246 0, 92pp, spined; cover: ld shako, chasseur and infantryman by the author, design by Mike Smith, orange blue and black. 7000 copies.

187. *Discovering Famous Battles: Ancient Warfare* Jeff Fletcher, 1974, 0 85263 247 9, 56pp, spined; cover: photo classic frieze, design by Robin Ollington, beige red and black. 4900 copies.

188. *Discovering Magic Charms and Talismans* Geoffrey Lamb, 1974, 0 85263 256 8, 48pp, spined; cover: ld pentacle by Robin Ollington, blue pink and black. 4900 copies.

189. *Discovering Geology* Patrick H. Armstrong, 1974, 0 85263 255 X, 64pp, spined; cover: ld fossils by Michael Hadley, black green and yellow. 7400 copies. 2nd ed, 1978, 0 85263 409 9.

190. *Discovering Garden Insects and other Invertebrates* Anthony Wootton, 1975, 0 85263 259 2, 80pp, spined; cover: ld butterfly, caterpillar by Richard Lewington, green and black. 4800 copies.

191. *Discovering Walks in the Cotswolds* Ronald Kershaw and Brian Robson, 1974, 0 85263 260 6, 64pp, stitched; cover: ld stile and village in oval by Edward Stamp, yellow brown blue and black. 4900 copies. 2nd ed, 1976, 0 85263 330 0. 1979, spined. 3rd ed, 1983, 0 85263 646 6; new cover: cp Calcot. 4th ed, 1989, 0 85263 992 9.

192. *Discovering Cambridgeshire* Margaret Turner, 1975, 0 85263 269 X, 52pp, stitched; cover: cartouche above engraving of Ely, green and black. 7500 copies.

193. *Discovering Northumbria* Harold Wade, 1975, 0 85263 270 3, 56pp, stitched; cover: cartouche above engraving of Jarrow, yellow and black. 6000 copies.

194. *Discovering Horse-drawn Carriages* D. J. Smith, 1974, 0 85263 286 X, 80pp, spined; cover: photo Victoria, design by Robin Ollington, purple brown and black. 7500 copies. 2nd ed, 1980, 0 85263 486 2. 3rd ed, 1985, 0 85263 720 9; new cover: cp Rothschild posting chariot.

195. *Discovering the Quantocks* Berta Lawrence, 1974, 0 85263 277 0, 48pp, stitched; cover: cartouche above engraving of Enmore Castle, pink and black. 4800 copies. 2nd ed, 1977, 0 85263 364 5. 3rd ed, 1980, 0 85263 526 5; new cover: cp ponies on Quantocks by Douglas Allen. 4th ed, 1984, 0 85263 660 1.

196. *Discovering the Folklore and Customs of Love and Marriage* Margaret Baker, 1974, 0 85263 280 0, 64pp, spined; cover: ld sweep and love tokens by Felix Partridge, purple yellow and black. 9900 copies.

197. *Discovering Lakeland* A. Harry Griffin, 1974, 0 85263 282 7, 56pp, stitched; cover: cartouche above engraving of Ullswater, green and black. 7500 copies.

198. *Discovering Walks in Wessex Towns* R. L. P. and Dorothy M. Jowitt, 1974, 0 85263 278 9, 144pp, spined; cover: ld townscape and footprints by Ron Shaddock, green yellow and black. 6900 copies.

199. *Discovering Corn Dollies* M. Lambeth, 1974, 0 85263 283 5, 48pp, spined; cover: ld Mother Earth and other dollies by R. C. Lambeth, design by Ron Shaddock, brown and black. 9900 copies. Reprinted.

200. *Discovering Mechanical Music* T. E. Crowley, 1975, 0 85263 257 6, 48pp, spined; cover: photo fairground organ figure, design by Robin Ollington, pink yellow and black. 5000 copies. 2nd ed, 1977, 0 85263 371 8.

201. *Discovering Backgammon* R. C. Bell, 1975, 0 85263 263 0, 48pp, spined; cover: photo Chinese backgammon set, design by Ron Shaddock, red and black. 5000 copies. 2nd ed, 1979, 0 85263 474 9.

202. *Discovering Bird Song* Edward A. Armstrong, 1975, 0 85263 291 6, 72pp, spined; cover: ld blackbird and sonagram by Ron Shaddock, green and black. 3900 copies. 2nd ed, 1977, 0 85263 395 3.

203. *Discovering South Yorkshire* John N. Merrill, 1975, 0 85263 298 3, 80pp, spined; cover: ld Conisbrough Castle by Ron Shaddock, green blue and black. 20,000 copies.

204. *Discovering Walks in Buckinghamshire* Ronald Pigram, 1975, 0 85263 299 1, 48pp, stitched; cover: ld stile and village in oval by Edward Stamp, green brown blue and black. 5000 copies.

205. *Discovering Kent* Marcus Crouch, 1975, 0 85263 300 9, 72pp, stitched; cover: cartouche above engraving of Barfreston church, green and black. 9000 copies.

206. *Discovering English Folk Dance* Hugh Rippon, 1975, 0 85263 271 1, 64pp, spined; cover:

253. *Discovering Preserved Railways* F. G. Cockman, 1980, 0 85263 515 X, 80pp, spined; cover: print steam engine in flood. 9800 copies. 2nd ed, 1985, 0 85263 723 3. 3rd ed, 1990, 0 7478 0073 1, 84pp.

254. *Discovering Shrines and Holy Places* David Pepin, 1980, 0 85263 514 1, 80pp, spined; cover: aquatint 'Christchurch Priory' from *Voyage Round Great Britain* by W. Daniell.

255. *Discovering Dice and Dominoes* R. C. Bell, 1980, 0 85263 532 X, 48pp, spined; cover: photo dominoes, dice and shaker, design by Ron Shaddock, black and brown.

256. *Discovering Backpacking* Ken Ward, 1980, 0 85263 466 8, 48pp, spined; cover: pen and wash backpackers above valley, by the author. 7000 copies.

257. *Discovering Canals in Britain* Peter L. Smith, 1981, 0 85263 549 4, 96pp, spined; cover: cp Grand Union Canal at Bulbourne. 7500 copies. 2nd ed, 1984, 0 85263 693 8. 3rd ed, 1989, 0 7478 0043 X.

258. *Discovering Horse-drawn Caravans* D. J. Smith, 1981, 0 85263 565 6, 64pp, spined; cover: cp Burton caravan by Lesley Watkinson. 9500 copies.

259. *Discovering London's Parks and Squares* John Wittich, 1981, 0 85263 550 8, 64pp, spined; cover: cp Battersea Park. 7200 copies.

260. *Discovering Old Cameras* Robert White, 1981, 0 85263 542 7, 88pp, spined; cover: cp four cameras by the author. 7000 copies. 2nd ed, 1984, 0 85263 691 1.

261. *Discovering Textile History and Design* K. G. Ponting, 1981, 0 85263 551 6, 72pp, spined; cover: cp detail of Devonshire Tapestry. 7300 copies. Reprinted.

262. *Discovering Traditional Farm Buildings* J. E. C. Peters, 1981, 0 85263 556 7, 80pp, spined; cover: cp farm buildings near Great Malvern by the author. 7200 copies. Reprinted.

263. *Discovering Walks in Suffolk* ed. John Andrews, 1981, 0 85263 559 1, 64pp, spined; cover: cp Southwold by Jeffery W. Whitelaw. 7400 copies.

264. *Discovering Walks in Surrey* Angela Haine and Susan Owen, 1981, 0 85263 560 5, 64pp, spined; cover: cp Shere. 4300 copies. 2nd ed, 1990, 0 7478 0072 3, 60pp.

265. *Discovering Lost Mines* Peter Naylor, 1981, 0 85263 544 3, 64pp, spined; cover: cp Watt's shaft beam engine house. 7200 copies.

266. *Discovering Antique Prints* Ronald Russell, 1982, 0 85263 587 7, 88pp, spined; cover: aquatint Llyn Ogween, after Loutherbourg. 7000 copies. Reprinted.

267. *Discovering Book Collecting* John Chidley, 1982, 0 85263 588 5, 80pp, spined; cover: cp bookshelves by John Slaughter. 7200 copies. Reprinted.

268. *Discovering Churchyards* Mark Child, 1982, 0 85263 603 2, 80pp, spined; cover: cp Penn churchyard. 7300 copies. Reprinted.

269. *Discovering English Vineyards* John R. Bedford, 1982, 0 85263 604 0, 56pp, spined; cover: cp vineyard at Brympton d'Evercy. 7100 copies.

270. *Discovering English Folksong* Michael Pollard, 1982, 0 85263 609 1, 48pp, spined; cover: coloured song sheet 'Fanny blooming fair'.

271. *Discovering Country Walks in South London* Susan Owen and Angela Haine, 1982, 0 85263 610 5, 64pp, spined; cover: cp Petersham Meadows. 6800 copies. 2nd ed, 1991, 0 7478 0114 2.

272. *Discovering Roman Britain* ed. David Johnston, 1983, 0 85263 627 X, 160pp, spined; cover: cp pavements at Fishbourne palace. 7500 copies.

273. *Discovering Walks in Essex* Derek Keeble, 1983, 0 85263 643 1, 56pp, spined; cover: cp Oliver's Footbridge near Colchester. 7500 copies.

274. *Discovering Walks in Norfolk* David Kennett, 1985, 0 85263 644 X, 56pp, spined; cover: cp Salthouse.

275. *Discovering Cottage Architecture* Christopher Powell, 1984, 0 85263 673 3, 104pp, spined; cover: cp cottage at Croyde. 7400 copies. Reprinted.

276. *Discovering English Watercolours* Alison Ambrose, 1987, 0 85263 902 3, 96pp, spined; cover: watercolour 'The Rabbit Hutch' by Walter Goodall.

277. *Discovering Walks in Lakeland Mountains* Don Hinson, 1985, 0 85263 717 9, 64pp, spined; cover: cp approach to Coniston Old Man.

278. *Discovering Scottish Architecture* T. W. West, 1985, 0 85263 748 9, 128pp, spined; cover: cp Drumlanrig Castle.

279. *Discovering Scottish Castles* Mike Salter, 1985, 0 85263 749 7, 160pp, spined; cover: cp Caerlaverock Castle.

280. *Discovering Avebury* Ian Edelman, 1985, 0 85263 766 7, 24pp, stitched; cover: cp village and south-west bank. 5000 copies. Reprinted.

281. *Discovering London Ceremonial and Traditions* Julian Paget, 1989, 0 85263 994 5, 72pp, spined; cover: cp guards on parade.

282. *Discovering Parish Boundaries* Angus Winchester, 1990, 0 7478 0060 X, 88pp, spined; cover: cp boundary stone between Ingleton and Bentham.

232. *Discovering London's Canals* Derek Pratt, 1977, 0 85263 396 3, 56pp, spined; cover: ld narrow-boat and zoo by Ron Shaddock, blue red and green. 7700 copies. 2nd ed, 1981, 0 85263 552 4. 3rd ed, 1987, 0 85263 901 5; new cover: cp 'Jason' on Regent's Canal by the author.

233. *Discovering Horse-drawn Transport of the British Army* D. J. Smith, 1977, 0 85263 403 X, 72pp, spined; cover: photo horse ambulance, design by Robin Ollington, yellow red and black. 4600 copies.

234. *Discovering Cleveland* Robert Woodhouse, 1978, 0 85263 412 9, 64pp, spined; cover: cp Tees estuary. 7300 copies.

235. *Discovering English Dialects* Martyn Wakelin, 1978, 0 85263 414 5, 64pp, spined; cover: ld five workers on map of England by Ron Shaddock, green blue and black. 5000 copies. 2nd ed, 1979, 0 85263 473 0.

236. *Discovering Bird Courtship* Edward A. Armstrong, 1978, 0 85263 415 3, 64pp, spined; cover: ld Jackson's whydah by R. A. Hume, ochre brown and black. 4000 copies.

237. *Discovering the Cinque Ports* C. E. Whitney, 1978, 0 85263 416 1, 64pp, spined; cover: cp Mermaid Street, Rye. 6000 copies. 2nd ed, 1988, 0 85263 914 7; new cover: cp Dover Castle.

238. *Discovering Farmhouse Cheese* Michael Cooper, 1978, 0 85263 417 X, 48pp, spined; cover: ld cheese room by the author, yellow green and black. 7200 copies.

239. *Discovering Walks in West Kent* Marcus Crouch, 1978, 0 85263 418 8, 56pp, stitched; cover: ld stile and village in oval by Edward Stamp, blue brown yellow and black. 7300 copies.

240. *Discovering Country Walks in North London* Merry Lundow, 1978, 0 85263 420 X, 72pp, spined; cover: ld fox, rabbit and traffic by Ron Shaddock, green red and black. 7100 copies. 2nd ed, 1981, 0 85263 574 5. 3rd ed, 1988, 0 85263 915 5.

241. *Discovering Nottinghamshire* Joan P. Alcock, 1978, 0 85263 426 9, 56pp, stitched; cover: cp Newstead Abbey. 5100 copies.

242. *Discovering Timber-framed Buildings* Richard Harris, 1978, 0 85263 427 7, 96pp, spined; cover: ld decorated frontages by the author, brown buff orange and black. 8500 copies. 2nd ed, 1979, 0 85263 481 1.

243. *Discovering London's Inns and Taverns* John Wittich, 1978, 0 85263 433 1, 64pp, spined; cover: ld cityscape with pubs by Ron Shaddock, red yellow and black. 9900 copies. 2nd ed, 1986, 0 85263 757 8; new cover: print of inn yard by Cecil Aldin.

244. *Discovering English Architecture* T. W. West, 1979, 0 85263 455 2, 128pp, spined; cover: ld Ashdown House by Ron Shaddock, green brown and black. 10,000 copies. 1984; new cover: cp Marble Hill House.

245. *Discovering Horse-drawn Farm Machinery* D. J. Smith, 1979, 0 85263 464 1, 96pp, spined;

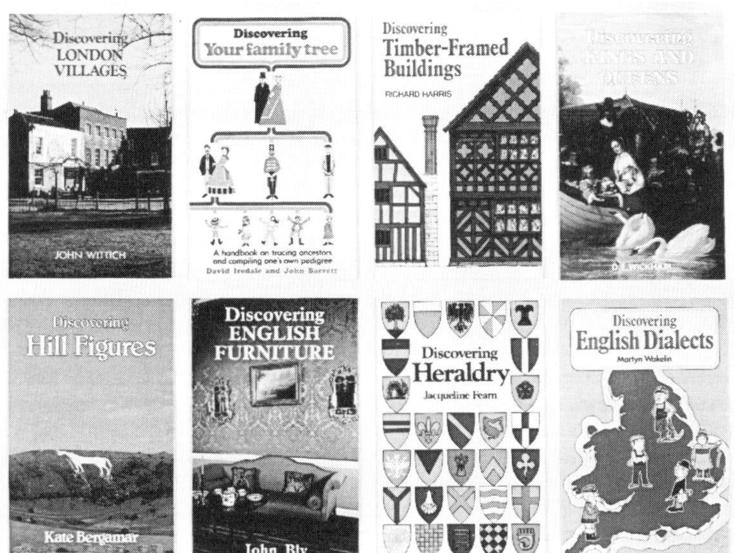

cover ld horse-drawn cultivator by Robin Ollington, yellow red and black. 9000 copies. 2nd ed, 1984, 0 85263 664 4; new cover: cp demonstration of self-delivery reaper.

246. *Discovering Farm Livestock* Nigel Harvey, 1979, 0 85263 465 X, 80pp, spined; ld farm animals and young by Ron Shaddock, green brown pink and black. 7100 copies.

247. *Discovering Treasure Hunting* C. W. Hill, 1980, 0 85263 489 7, 64pp, spined; cover: ld spade and finds by Ron Shaddock, brown blue and black. 7000 copies.

248. *Discovering Walking* H. D. Westacott, 1979, 0 85263 467 6, 56pp, spined; cover: ld family group in hills by Ron Shaddock, green red blue and black. 5800 copies.

249. *Discovering Country Winemaking* Daphne More, 1980, 0 85263 480 3, 64pp, spined; cover: ld fruit-filled jar by Ron Shaddock, red green yellow and black. 9600 copies. Reprinted.

250. *Discovering Heraldry* Jacqueline Fearn, 1980, 0 85263 476 5, 96pp, spined; cover: ld heraldic shields by Ron Shaddock, yellow red blue green and black. 9800 copies. 1983; cover change: colours altered.

251. *Discovering Dowsing and Divining* Peter Naylor, 1980, 0 85263 516 8, 40pp, spined; cover: ld hands with twig by Ron Shaddock, green brown and black. 9700 copies. Reprinted.

252. *Discovering the North Downs Way* David J. Allen and Patrick R. Imrie, 1980, 0 85263 512 5, 80pp, spined; cover: cp Trottiscliffe church. 7200 copies. 2nd ed, 1987, 0 85263 844 1.

Lifelines 16
Will Adams

ALMA-
TADEMA

ERNEST
BEVIN
Richard Tames

Thomas
Brassey
Jack Gould

Lifelines 14
JAMES
BRINDLEY

BURNE-JONES

Lifelines 27
Alice M. Coats
Lord Bute

Lifelines 22
GEORGE
CADBURY
Bournville
Walter Stranz

Lifelines 11
Joseph
Chamberlain
C.W. Hill
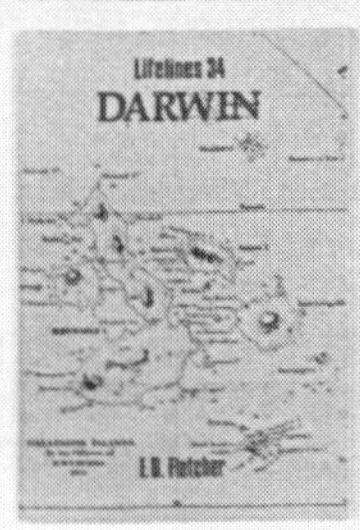
Lifelines 34
DARWIN

FOX
TALBOT
John Hannavy

Lifelines 13
GILLRAY AND
CRUIKSHANK
Michael
Katanka
and
Edgell
Rickword

Lifelines 2
GENERAL
GORDON
Richard Tames

John
Hampden

Richard Tames
Hitler

Ebenezer
HOWARD

Lifelines 37
Gertrude
Jekyll

Lifelines 25
KITCHENER
BRITONS
YOU
JOIN YOUR COUNTRY'S ARMY!
GOD SAVE THE KING
R.J. Wilkinson-Latham

Lifelines 20
LANDSEER

Lifelines 35
Joseph
LOCKE
Charles
Walker

Lifelines 3
WILLIAM
MORRIS

ISAAC NEWTON

Mungo Park
RICHARD TAMES

Lifelines 21
PAXTON
John Anthony

LIFELINES

'Lifelines' is a series of illustrated biographies, first published in 1972. They are A5 format (215 mm by 150 mm), are all 48 pages in length and square-backed with spines. They are numbered on the front cover and on the spine. Several titles were withdrawn because of faulty binding; hence the small quantities of some titles in circulation.

1. *Isambard Kingdom Brunel* Richard Tames, 1972, 0 85263 140 5; cover: photo Brunel in front of anchor chains, design by Robin Ollington, brown blue and black. 7300 copies. Reprinted 1975 but no change to verso. Back cover lists 37 titles with prices. All further reprints have verso amended.

2. *General Gordon* Richard Tames, 1972, 0 85263 141 3; cover: death of Gordon, design by Robin Ollington, red black brown and blue. 4700 copies.

3. *William Morris* Richard Tames, 1972, 0 85263 142 1; cover: sepia photo of Morris in Kelmscott Press border, design by Robin Ollington, green brown and black. 7000 copies. 1987; new cover: Morris design 'Lodden' as border, photo black.

4. *Josiah Wedgwood* Richard Tames, 1972, 0 85263 143 X; cover: Jasper portrait of Wedgwood against ld Churchyard Works, design by Robin Ollington, brown blue and black. 6600 copies. 1987; new cover: portrait Josiah Wedgwood by George Stubbs.

5. *Cecil Rhodes* Richard Tames, 1973, 0 85263 175 8; cover: *Punch* cartoon 'The Rhodes Colossus', design by Robin Ollington, green pink and black. 1800 copies.

6. *Richard Trevithick* James Hodge, 1973, 0 85263 177 4; cover: engraving of portrait of Trevithick by Linnell and 1803 locomotive, design by Robin Ollington, black brown and green. 4600 copies. 1978; cover change: green omitted. 1989; new cover: portrait of Trevithick by J. Linnell, 1816.

7. *Henry Morton Stanley* Richard Tames, 1973, 0 85263 176 6; cover: photo of Stanley and engraving of meeting with Livingstone, design by Robin Ollington, green brown and black. 4000 copies.

8. *Robert Stephenson* Donald J. Smith, 1973, 0 85263 186 3; cover: locomotive and engraved portrait, design by Robin Ollington, green beige and black. 4900 copies. 1987; new cover: cp High Level Bridge, Newcastle upon Tyne.

9. *Bulwer-Lytton* Sibylla Jane Flower, 1973, 0 85263 187 1; cover: cartoon of Bulwer-Lytton by Ape, design by Robin Ollington, blue red and black. 4300 copies.

10. *Thomas Telford* Rhoda M. Pearce, 1973, 0 85263 188 X; cover: engraving of Pontcysyllte Aqueduct and medallion portrait, design by Robin Ollington, brown blue and black. 4800 copies. 2nd ed 1978, 0 85263 410 2. 1987; new cover: cp Pontcysyllte Aqueduct.

11. *Joseph Chamberlain* C. W. Hill, 1973, 0 85263 174 X; cover: cartoon portrait in 'coat of many colours', design by Robin Ollington, blue red yellow orange black. 3400 copies.

12. *Burne-Jones* William Waters, 1973, 0 85263 199 5; cover: photo Burne-Jones on artist's

steps, design by Robin Ollington, blue red and black. 4200 copies. 1984; cover change: yellow red and black. Date of reprint omitted. 1989; new cover: painting 'Laus Veneris'.

13. *Gillray and Cruikshank* Michael Katanka and Edgell Rickword, 1973, 0 85263 200 2; cover: ld 'John Bull taking a Luncheon' by Gillray, beige red and black. 1600 copies.

14. *James Brindley* Harold Bode, 1973, 0 85263 201 0; cover: engraved portrait of Brindley and map of Bridgewater Canal, cream red and black. 4500 copies. 2nd ed, 1980, 0 85263 485 4. 1987; new cover: cp Tackley Bridge by Derek Pratt.

15. *John Ruskin* James S. Dearden, 1973, 0 85263 202 9; cover: pen and wash caricature of Ruskin as the Angel of Light, designed by Michael Hadley, blue brown and black. 3700 copies.

16. *Will Adams* Richard Tames, 1973, 0 85263 203 7; cover: pen and wash portrait of Adams with chart by Michael Hadley, blues and black. 1000 copies.

17. *Pugin* John Harries, 1973, 0 85263 204 5; cover: pen and wash portrait of Pugin in Gothic arch by Michael Hadley, pink red and black. 1700 copies.

18. *Ebenezer Howard* John Moss-Eccardt, 1973, 0 85263 205 3; cover: pen and wash portrait of Howard and map of Letchworth by Michael Hadley, red green and black. 4800 copies.

19. *Mungo Park* Richard Tames, 1973, 0 85263 206 1; cover: pen and wash portrait of Park and African tribesmen by Michael Hadley, yellow brown and black. 1300 copies.

20. *Landseer* Ian Barras Hill, 1973, 0 85263 207 X; cover: Landseer and 'Monarch of the Glen', design by Robin Ollington, brown blue and black. 3800 copies.

21. *Joseph Paxton* John Anthony, 1973, 0 85263 208 8; cover: portrait of Paxton by Octavius Oakley and the Crystal Palace, design by Robin Ollington, brown blue and black. 4100 copies. Reprinted.

22. *George Cadbury* Walter Stranz, 1973, 0 85263 236 3; cover: photo of Cadbury and map of Bournville, design by Robin Ollington, chocolate blue and black. 4100 copies.

23. *Zeppelin* T. E. Guttery, 1973, 0 85263 210 X; cover: Count Zeppelin and airship, design by Robin Ollington, silver blue and black. 4100 copies.

24. *Alma-Tadema* Russell Ash, 1973, 0 85263 237 1; cover: 'In the Tepidarium' and photo of Alma-Tadema, design by Robin Ollington, cream purple and black. 1400 copies.

25. *Kitchener* R. J. Wilkinson-Latham, 1973, 0 85263 238 X; cover: recruiting poster and recruits, design by Robin Ollington; brown red and black. 1700 copies.

26. *Wellington* Amoret and Christopher Scott, 1973, 0 85263 239 8, cover: ld 'A Wellington Boot', design by Robin Ollington, red yellow and black. 4800 copies. Reprinted.

27. *Lord Bute* Alice M. Coats, 1975, 0 85263 272 X; Lord Bute by Allan Ramsay and *Stewartia malacodendron*, design by Ron Shaddock, green purple and black. 2500 copies.

28. *Humphry Repton* Kay N. Sanecki, 1974, 0 85263 273 8; cover: ld figures from Repton's trade card, brown and black. 2500 copies. 1987; new cover: watercolour detail from Red Book for Ashridge.

29. *Ernest Bevin* Richard Tames, 1974, 0 85263 248 7; cover: photo Bevin and horse delivery van during the General Strike, design by Ron Shaddock, brown red and black. 3000 copies.

30. *Hitler* Richard Tames, 1974, 0 85263 249 5; cover: photo Hitler against swastika flag by Ron Shaddock, black and red. 4700 copies.

31. *Joseph Priestley* A. D. Orange, 1974, 0 85263 252 5; cover: pen and wash Priestley and rioting mob by Michael Hadley, blue red and black. 4000 copies.

32. *Sir Winston Churchill* Richard Tames, 1974, 0 85263 253 3; cover: photo Churchill, blue red and black. 2000 copies.

33. *Capability Brown* Joan Clifford, 1974, 0 85263 274 6; cover: engraving Danson Park, green and black. 2400 copies. 1983; cover change: beige and black. 1987; new cover: cp Bowood lake.

34. *Darwin* F. D. Fletcher, 1975, 0 85263 293 2; cover: ld map of Galapagos Islands, blues and black. 2200 copies. 2nd ed, 1980, 0 85263 523 0. 1988; new cover: oil portrait of Darwin by the Honourable John Collier.

35. *Joseph Locke* Charles Walker, 1975, 0 85263 294 0; cover: portrait of Locke and locomotive, green and black. 2200 copies.

36. *Thomas Brassey* Jack Gould, 1975, 0 85263 295 9; cover: engraving Mont Cenis Summit Railway, blue and black. 2200 copies.

37. *Gertrude Jekyll* Betty Massingham, 1975, 0 85263 304 1; cover: ld Munstead Wood by Richard Lewington, green and black. 2500 copies. 1987, new cover: cp Hestercombe House gardens by Iris Hardwick.

38. *Fox Talbot* John Hannavy, 1976, 0 85263 319 X; cover: photo Talbot's photographic premises at Reading, yellow and black. 2500 copies. 2nd ed, 1984, 0 85263 645 8; cover change: cream red and black. 1987; new cover: cp Lacock Abbey by the author.

39. *Lord Nuffield* Peter Hull, 1977, 0 85263 397 1; cover: photo Nuffield and car assembly line, design by Ron Shaddock, pink crimson and black. 5600 copies.

40. *John Hampden* Frank Hansford-Miller, 1976, 0 85263 322 X; cover: engraved portrait of Hampden and Saxton's map of Buckinghamshire, brown and black. 2200 copies.

41. *Isaac Newton* Colin A. Ronan, 1976, 0 85263 323 8; cover: engraved portrait of Newton and Woolsthorpe Manor, rose and black. 2400 copies.

42. *Vanbrugh* John Anthony, 1977, 0 85263 339 4; cover: engraving Castle Howard, violet and black. 2100 copies.

The first sixteen Shire Albums, published between 1973 and 1976.

SHIRE ALBUMS

Shire Albums were first published in 1973. They illustrate architectural, collecting, domestic, industrial, rural and social themes using black and white photographs, engravings and line drawings and an accompanying text of about 5000 words. They are A5 format (215 mm by 150 mm), are all 32 pages in length, and are saddle-stitched in the centrefold with two wires. Early printings of the first 54 titles carried illustrations or text on the inside covers. Numbers 1 to 43 had two-colour covers dominated by a large wreath which enclosed the series number, the title and the author. Titles 44 and 46 adopted an oblong title panel but still used two colours. Titles 45, 47 and all subsequent to these bear an oblong coloured title panel in which the original wreath design, much reduced, holds the series number. The panel is set above or is reversed out of a full-colour illustration. In subsequent printings of those titles which had two-colour covers, the cover has been changed to the new design with full-colour illustrations.

1. *Vintage Farm Machines* John Vince, 1973, 0 85263 225 8; cover: photo steam threshing scene, design by Robin Ollington, blue and black. 10,500 copies. 2nd ed, 1978, 0 85263 440 4.

2. *Fire-marks* John Vince, 1973, 0 85263 226 6; cover: photo fire-marks, design by Robin Ollington, yellow and black. 7200 copies. 1983; new cover: cp County Fire Office fire plate.

3. *Canals and Canal Architecture* John Vince, 1973, 0 85263 229 0; cover: photo Bingley Five-rise locks by Ivan E. Broadhead, blue and black. 9700 copies. Revised (2nd) edition, 1976, 0 85263 353 X; cover change: green and black.

4. *Old Farm Tools* John Vince, 1974, 0 85263 275 4; cover: tools in reversed silhouette and photo by Ron Shaddock, green and black. 7000 copies. 1980; new cover: cp publisher with seed fiddle and tools by the author.

5. *Old British Livestock* John Vince, 1974, 0 85263 276 2; cover: photo montage of farm animals by Ron Shaddock, brown and black. 7000 copies. Revised (2nd) edition, 1976, 0 85263 346 7.

6. *Bottles and Bottle Collecting* A. A. C. Hedges, 1975, 0 85263 209 6; cover: photo Victorian bottles and jars by the author, green and black. 7200 copies. (1980) sixth impression; new cover: cp bottles and jars in three rows by the author.

7. *Haunted Houses* Andrew Green, 1975, 0 85263 292 4; cover: Warley Abbey by Ron Shaddock, purple and black. 9300 copies. 2nd ed, 1979, 0 85263 460 9. 1985: new cover: watercolour Gothick house by Grahame Tomkins.

8. *Canal Barges and Narrow Boats* Peter L. Smith, 1975, 0 85263 311 4; cover: photo montage of boats by Ron Shaddock, blue and black. 9100 copies. 2nd ed, 1979, 0 85263 463 3; new cover: photo narrow boats at Iron Bridge lock, Watford, blue and black. 3rd ed, 1983, 0 85263 651 2; new cover: cp narrow boat 'Ascot' at Braunston by the author. 4th ed, 1986, 0 85263 794 2.

9. *Pillow Lace and Bobbins* Jeffery Hopewell, 1975, 0 85263 312 2; cover: photo lace and bobbins by S. T. Bindley, blue and black. 7500 copies. 2nd ed, 1977, 0 85263 408 0. 1980; new cover: cp lace, bobbins and parchment by S. T. Bindley. 3rd ed, 1984, 0 85263 659 8.

10. *Old Farm Buildings* Nigel Harvey, 1975, 0 85263 313 0; cover: photo barn at Old Knebworth, orange and black. 7300 copies. 2nd ed, 1977, 0 85263 351 3. 1980; new cover: cp Great Coxwell tithe barn. 3rd ed, 1987, 0 85263 865 5.

11. *The Village Wheelwright and Carpenter* Jocelyn Bailey, 1975, 0 85263 314 9; cover: photo wagon wheel, green and black. 7400 copies. 1977, 0 85263 394 7. This second impression given new ISBN on cover although original ISBN shown on verso. Subsequent impressions show new ISBN. 1980; new cover: cp wheelwright at work.

12. *Inn Signs* Cadbury Lamb, 1976, 0 85263 327 0; cover: photo Green Man sign from Harlow, design by Ron Shaddock, blue and black. 9500 copies. 1980; new cover: cp former Queen's Head sign, Long Marston, Hertfordshire.

13. *Sailing Barges* Martin Hazell, 1976, 0 85263 334 3; cover: photo barge 'Pudge' in the Colne, blue and black. 7600 copies. 2nd ed, 1982, 0 85263 584 2; new cover: cp barge viewed through rigging by Peter Ferguson. 1986; new cover: cp barge in full sail by Peter Ferguson.

14. *Railway Architecture* F. G. Cockman, 1976, 0 85263 335 1; cover: photo Tamar viaduct by the author, grey and black. 9600 copies. 2nd ed, 1988, 0 85263 917 1; new cover: cp Tamar viaduct by the author.

15. *Beam Engines* T. E. Crowley, 1976, 0 85263 336 X; cover: photo Adam Heslop engine in Science Museum, brown and black. 6700 copies. 2nd ed, 1978, 0 85263 430 7. 3rd ed, 1982, 0 85263 595 8; new cover: cp Easton, Amos engine at City of Birmingham Museum of Science and Industry by J. H. Andrew. 4th ed, 1986, 0 85263 802 7.

16. *Thatch and Thatching* Jacqueline Fearn, 1976, 0 85263 337 8; cover: photo thatcher using a leggatt, brown and black. 7500 copies. 1978; new cover: photo thatcher on ladder, brown and black. 1981; new cover: mezzotint 'The Thatcher' by G. Morland.

17. *Travelling Fairs* David Braithwaite, 1976, 0 85263 338 6; cover: photo horse on gallopers, red and black. 7500 copies.

18. *Craft Pottery* Thomas Plowman, 1976, 0 85263 347 5; cover: photo contents of a bisque kiln by the author, brown and black. 7500 copies. 1980; new cover: cp pottery candle holder by the author.

19. *Old Horseshoes* Ivan G. Sparkes, 1976, 0 85263 348 3; cover: page from Samuel Lewis catalogue, *c.*1920, purple and black. 4900 copies. 1983; new cover: print 'Shoeing the Bay Mare' by Landseer.

20. *Domestic Bygones* Jacqueline Fearn, 1977, 0 85263 349 1; cover: photo montage of bygones by Ron Shaddock, pink and black. 10,000 copies. 1980; new cover: cp inglenook fireplace with equipment.

21. *Fields, Hedges and Ditches* Nigel Harvey, 1976, 0 85263 350 5; cover: photo fields near

Ellesborough by Mary Farnell, green and black. 7500 copies. 2nd ed, 1987, 0 85263 868 X; new cover: cp Hundred Acre Field, Ellesborough.

22. *Curious England* Eileen Preston, 1977, 0 85263 360 2; cover: photo montage by Ron Shaddock, purple and black. 6600 copies. 1985; new cover: cp topiary church at Stratford sub Castle by the author.

23. *Shepherding Tools and Customs* Arthur Ingram, 1977, 0 85263 379 3; cover: photo Victorian shepherd and dog, brown and black. 9900 copies. 1983; new cover: watercolour 'Sheep Shearing' by Frederick Taylor.

24. *The Village Blacksmith* Jocelyn Bailey, 1977, 0 85263 380 7; cover: photo blacksmith Roger Mildred at Mentmore by Michael Bass, red and black. 2nd ed, 1980, 0 85263 511 7; new cover: cp Roger Mildred by Michael Bass.

25. *Woodland Craftsmen* Ivan G. Sparkes, 1977, 0 85263 381 5; cover: photo bodger's hut, green and black. 10,100 copies. 1991; new cover: cp besom maker.

26. *Farms and Farming* Nigel Harvey, 1977, 0 85263 382 3; cover: photo farmhouse and cornfield by Raymond Lea, olive and black. 9900 copies.

Shire Albums 17-24, published 1976-7.

27. *Occupational Costume* Avril Lansdell, 1977, 0 85263 383 1; cover: ld five occupations by Ron Shaddock, green and black. 7700 copies. 1984; new cover: painting 'St James's Fair' by Samuel Coleman.

28. *The Village Cooper* K. Kilby, 1977, 0 85263 392 0; cover: photo cooperage, brown and black. 7400 copies. 1983; new cover: cp cooper at Museum of Cider, Hereford.

29. *Dairying Bygones* Arthur Ingram, 1977, 0 85263 393 9; cover: mezzotint 'The Dairy Farm' by James Ward, yellow and black. 7400 copies. 1980; new cover: cp 'The Dairy Farm' by James Ward. 2nd ed, 1987, 0 85263 866 3.

30. *Samplers* Pamela Clabburn, 1977, 0 85263 407 2; cover: sampler 1837 by Eliza Richardson, pink and black. 7600 copies. 1980; new cover: cp sampler 1834 by Temperance Fisher.

31. *Fisherman Knitting* Michael Harvey and Rae Compton, 1978, 0 85263 421 8; cover: photo four Sheringham fishermen 1910, blue and black. 7600 copies. 1982; cover change: wreath replaced by oblong title panel. 1985: cover change: photo enlarged to show only three fishermen.

32. *The Victorian Ironmonger* Cecil A. Meadows, 1978, 0 85263 422 6; cover: pen and wash ironmonger's shop by Ron Shaddock, brown and black. 7400 copies. 2nd ed, 1984, 0 85263 704 7; new cover: watercolour of ironmonger's shop by Grahame Tomkins.

33. *Mills and Millwrighting* John Vince, 1978, 0 85263 431 5; cover: photo millwright dressing stones, buff and black. 9800 copies.

34. *Trapping and Poaching* Arthur Ingram, 1978, 0 85263 432 3; cover: photo traps, design by Ron Shaddock, green and black. 7500 copies. 1984, new cover: hand-coloured engraving of poachers.

35. *Old Poultry Breeds* Fred Hams, 1978, 0 85263 434 X; cover: print 'Boys Own Hen Yard' 1897, rose and black. 7400 copies. 2nd ed, 1983, 0 85263 655 5; new cover: coloured print 'Boys Own Hen Yard'.

36. *Wells and Water Supply* John Vince, 1978, 0 85263 441 2; cover: ld bucket descending well by Ron Shaddock, blue and black. 7000 copies.

37. *Clay Tobacco Pipes* Eric G. Ayto, 1979, 0 85263 450 1; cover: photo three clay pipes, brown and black. 7100 copies. 1984; cover change: wreath replaced by oblong title panel. 2nd ed, 1987, 0 85263 863 9.

38. *Needlework Tools* Eleanor Johnson, 1978, 0 85263 446 3; cover: photo montage of tools by Ron Shaddock, brown and black. 1980; new cover: cp sewing work table with tools.

39. *The Heavy Horse* Edward Hart, 1979, 0 85263 452 8; cover: photo heads of pair of greys by Michael Bass, beige and black. 1981; new cover: cp a Percheron drawing an Oxfordshire wagon.

40. *The Country Animal Doctor* Arthur Ingram, 1979, 0 85263 462 5; cover: photo of old

veterinary tools by Malcolm Harris, red and black. 7300 copies.

41. *Old Garden Tools* Kay N. Sanecki, 1979, 0 85263 470 6; cover: ld tools from John Evelyn's *Elysium Britannicum*, green and black. 7400 copies. 2nd ed, 1987, 0 85263 869 8; new cover: oil painting 'Smithills Hall from the South' *c*.1840.

42. *Stationary Steam Engines* Geoffrey Hayes, 1979, 0 85263 453 6; cover: photo engine at Dee spinning mill by the author, grey and black. 7400 copies. 2nd ed, 1983, 0 85263 652 0; new cover: cp winding engine at Lady Victoria Colliery by the author.

43. *Spinning and Spinning Wheels* Eliza Leadbeater, 1979, 0 85263 469 2; cover: photo author spinning in field, green and black. 9800 copies. 1981; new cover: oil painting 'The Spinstress' by George Romney.

44. *Weights and Measures* J. T. Graham, 1979, 0 85263 479 X; cover: photo montage of weights by Ron Shaddock, olive and black. 7300 copies. 2nd ed, 1987, 0 85263 867 1; new cover: cp two rows of weights and measures by David J. Stevenson.

45. *The Drovers* Shirley Toulson, 1980, 0 85263 505 2; cover: oil painting figures with cattle and sheep. 7000 copies. Reprinted.

46. *Smocks* Maggie Hall, 1979, 0 85263 477 3; cover: photo Dorset carter, design by Ron Shaddock, brown and black. 9700 copies. 1983; new cover: cp editor in modern smock made by author.

47. *Street Furniture* Henry Aaron, 1980, 0 85263 498 6; cover: cp gas lamp in Guildhall Yard, London, by Ian Sherren. 6900 copies. 2nd ed, 1987, 0 85263 864 7.

48. *Vintage Tractors* Charles L. Cawood, 1980, 0 85263 499 4; cover: cp 1903 Ivel tractor. 7200 copies. Reprinted.

49. *Old Stationary Engines* David W. Edgington, 1980, 0 85263 500 1; cover: cp Victoria engine. 6400 copies. Reprinted.

50. *Woodworking Tools* Philip Walker, 1980, 0 85263 501 X; cover: cp hewing axe, plane and brace. 9800 copies. Reprinted.

51. *Rope, Twine and Net Making* Anthony Sanctuary, 1980, 0 85263 502 8; cover: painting of cottagers making nets by Francis Newberry. 7000 copies. 2nd ed, 1988, 0 85263 918 X.

52. *Jet Jewellery and Ornaments* Helen Muller, 1980, 0 85263 503 6; cover: cp collarette necklace and cameo. 7500 copies. Reprinted.

53. *The Harness Horse* Edward Hart, 1981, 0 85263 504 4; cover: cp sociable in Royal Crescent, Bath, by Graham and Barbara Swanson. 7000 copies. Reprinted.

54. *Writing Antiques* George Mell, 1980, 0 85263 519 2; cover: cp writing slope with accessories. 6800 copies. Reprinted.

55. *Scales and Balances* J. T. Graham, 1981, 0 85263 547 8; cover: cp several scales and

balances. 7300 copies. 2nd ed, 1986, 0 85263 840 X.

56. *The Victorian Professional Photographer* John Hannavy, 1980, 0 85263 524 9; cover: watercolour of photographer with portable darkroom by Michael Taylor. 7100 copies.

57. *Beadwork* Pamela Clabburn, 1980, 0 85263 529 X; cover: cp bead reticule with sportsman and dog. 7300 copies. Reprinted.

58. *Fashion Accessories* Eleanor Johnson, 1980, 0 85263 530 3; cover: cp several accessories by Michael Bass. 7300 copies. Reprinted.

59. *Corkscrews and Bottle Openers* Evan Perry, 1980, 0 85263 534 6; cover: cp lever corkscrew in action. 7500 copies. Reprinted.

60. *Board and Table Game Antiques* R. C. Bell, 1981, 0 85263 538 9; cover: cp various small games items. 4300 copies. 1990; new cover: print 'Paddy Puzzled' by C. Hunt.

61. *Village and Town Bands* Christopher Weir, 1981, 0 85263 541 9; cover: oil painting 'The Village Choir' by Thomas Webster. 6300 copies.

62. *The Potteries* David Sekers, 1981, 0 85263 564 8; cover: watercolour 'Blue Bell Works' by Reginald Haggar. 6800 copies. Reprinted.

63. *The Cotton Industry* Chris Aspin, 1981, 0 85263 545 1; cover: oil painting 'The Dinner Hour, Wigan' by Eyre Crowe. 7000 copies. Reprinted.

64. *Ironworking* W. K. V. Gale, 1981, 0 85263 546 X; cover: 'Coalbrookdale by Night' by P. J. de Loutherbourg. 7400 copies. Reprinted.

65. *Gas Lighting* David Gledhill, 1981, 0 85263 539 7; cover: cp wall gas light. 7300 copies. Reprinted.

66. *Smoking Antiques* Amoret and Christopher Scott, 1981, 0 85263 540 0; cover: cp various tobacco-related items by Michael Bass. 7400 copies. Reprinted.

67. *Victorian Tiles* Hans van Lemmen, 1981, 0 85263 548 6; cover: cp single floral tile. 6800 copies. Reprinted.

68. *Fire Engines* Trevor Whitehead, 1981, 0 85263 555 9; cover: cp Leyland Cub pump escape. 7300 copies. Reprinted.

69. *Chains and Chainmaking* Charles Fogg, 1981, 0 85263 561 3; cover: cp chainmakers at work. 7300 copies.

70. *English Windsor Chairs* Ivan G. Sparkes, 1981, 0 85263 562 1; cover: print Edwin Skull's broadsheet of chairs. 7300 copies. Reprinted.

71. *Needlemaking* John G. Rollins, 1981, 0 85263 563 X; cover: cp author making needles. 7100 copies.

72. *Brewing and Breweries* Maurice Lovett, 1981, 0 85263 568 0; cover: print The Park Brewery, Wolverhampton. 7200 copies. Reprinted.

73. *Steel Ship Building* Fred M. Walker, 1981, 0 85263 569 9; cover: cp 'Glenfalloch' about to be launched at Govan. 7200 copies.

74. *Trees, Woods and Forests* Nigel Harvey, 1981, 0 85263 572 9; cover: watercolour 'A Lane in Kent' by William Bennett. 7300 copies.

75. *Bricks and Brickmaking* Martin Hammond, 1981, 0 85263 573 7; cover: cp sixteen types of brick by Philip T. Smith. 7300 copies. 2nd ed, 1990, 0 7478 0067 7.

76. *Straw and Straw Craftsmen* Arthur Staniforth, 1981, 0 85263 575 3; cover: cp making bee skeps from wheat straw. 7100 copies. 2nd ed, 1991, 0 7478 0103 7; cover change: title panel changed from green to brown.

77. *Shawls* Pamela Clabburn, 1981, 0 85263 579 6; cover: cp shawl by Towler and Campin of Norwich. 7400 copies. Reprinted.

78. *Straw Plait* Jean Davis, 1981, 0 85263 580 X; cover: cp straw hat and plaiting items by Mary Farnell. 6900 copies.

79. *Trade Tokens of the Industrial Revolution* Jim Newmark, 1981, 0 85263 582 6; cover: cp five tokens. 7000 copies.

80. *The Victorian Chemist and Druggist* W. A. Jackson, 1981, 0 85263 583 4; cover: cp specie jar, syrup bottle, eye-bath and paper folder by Michael Bass. 7400 copies. Reprinted.

81. *The Woollen Industry* Chris Aspin, 1982, 0 85263 598 2; cover: print 'Cloth Dressers' from *The Costume of Yorkshire*. 7400 copies. Reprinted.

82. *The Collier* A. R. Griffin, 1982, 0 85263 590 7; cover: print 'The Collier' from *The Costume of Yorkshire*. 7300 copies. Reprinted.

83. *Glass and Glassmaking* Roger Dodsworth, 1982, 0 85263 585 0; cover: oil painting 'The Richardson Glassworks, Wordsley, Stourbridge', *c.*1830 by Emily Hodgetts. 7300 copies. Reprinted.

84. *Old Sewing Machines* Carol Head, 1982, 0 85263 591 5; cover: cp 'free-arm' lock-stitch sewing machine by E. Ward, 1876. 6900 copies. Reprinted.

85. *Lead and Leadmining* Lynn Willies, 1982, 0 85263 596 6; cover: cp Stonedge cupola by the author. 7200 copies. Reprinted.

86. *Old Trade Handcarts* Gerry Backhouse, 1982, 0 85263 608 3; cover: cp ice-cream barrow. 7100 copies.

87. *Nailmaking* Hugh Bodey, 1983, 0 85263 606 7; cover: cp nailmaking at Tremont Nail Company, Massachusetts. 7100 copies.

88. *Ayrshire and other Whitework* Margaret Swain, 1982, 0 85263 589 3; cover: photo crown of baby cap, red and black. 7400 copies. Reprinted.

89. *Whales and Whaling* Arthur G. Credland, 1982, 0 85263 597 4; cover: oil painting 'The Swan and the Isabella' *c.*1825 by John Ward. 6100 copies.

90. *Cricketing Bygones* Stephen Green, 1982, 0 85263 605 9; cover: print cricket match at Rugby school 1889, after H. Jamyn Brooks. 7400 copies. Reprinted.

91. *Old Lawnmowers* David Halford, 1982, 0 85263 607 5; cover: cp Ransomes, Sims and Jefferies Mark 8 24-inch lawnmower. 7300 copies.

92. *Baskets and Basketmaking* Alastair Heseltine, 1982, 0 85263 611 3; cover: cp author making a basket. 7300 copies. Reprinted.

93. *Follies* Jeffery W. Whitelaw, 1982, 0 85263 612 1; cover: cp Old John Folly, Bradgate Park, by the author. 7100 copies. 2nd ed, 1990, 0 7478 0096 0.

94. *Old Buses* David Kaye, 1982, 0 85263 613 X; cover: cp London General Omnibus Company 'K' type, 1920. 7300 copies. Reprinted.

95. *Cidermaking* Michael B. Quinion, 1982, 0 85263 614 8; cover: cp hand-operated cider press. 7400 copies. Reprinted.

96. *Thimbles* Eleanor Johnson, 1982, 0 85263 619 9; cover: cp rows of thimbles by Michael Bass. 7400 copies. Reprinted.

97. *Blue and White Transfer-printed Pottery* Robert Copeland, 1982, 0 85263 620 2; cover: cp several pieces of pottery. 7500 copies. Reprinted

98. *Corn Milling* Martin Watts, 1983, 0 85263 623 7; cover: cp windmill at North Leverton. 7300 copies. Reprinted.

99. *Firegrates and Kitchen Ranges* David J. Eveleigh, 1983, 0 85263 629 6; cover: cp Hattersley range at Cogges. 7400 copies. Reprinted.

100. *Agricultural Hand Tools* Roy Brigden, 1983, 0 85263 630 X; cover: print showing autumn sowing, 1818, from drawing by J. M. W. Turner. 7400 copies. Reprinted.

101. *Patchwork* Pamela Clabburn, 1983, 0 85263 631 8; cover: cp Sudanese horse armour. 7300 copies. Reprinted.

102. *Toy Soldiers* James Opie, 1983, 0 85263 632 6; cover: cp procession of toy guardsmen by Michael Bass. 7400 copies. Reprinted.

103. *Textile Machines* Anna P. Benson, 1983, 0 85263 647 4; cover: cp Crompton's mule. 7300 copies. Reprinted.

104. *Carnival Glass* Raymond Notley, 1983, 0 85263 637 7; cover: cp range of glassware by the author. 7000 copies. 2nd ed, 1986, 0 85263 838 8. 3rd ed, 1990, 0 7478 0098 7.

105. *Clay and Cob Buildings* John McCann, 1983, 0 85263 638 5; cover: cp cottage of chalk cob at Orcheston by the author. 7900 copies.

106. *Coins and Minting* Denis Cooper, 1983, 0 85263 639 3; cover: cp medal depicting screw press in operation. 7300 copies. 2nd ed, 1990, 0 7478 0069 3. Verso has incorrect ISBN.

107. *Laundry Bygones* Pamela Sambrook, 1983, 0 85263 648 2; cover: cp laundry at Shugborough. 7300 copies. Reprinted.

108. *Lost Trade Routes* Shirley Toulson, 1983, 0 85263 649 0; cover: watercolour 'Llangwllais Pass, North Wales' by D. W. Haddon.

109. *Ships' Figureheads* M. K. Stammers, 1983, 0 85263 650 4; cover: cp Lord Nelson figurehead. 7300 copies. Reprinted.

110. *Anchors* N. E. Upham, 1983, 0 85263 636 9; cover: cp anchor wharf at National Maritime Museum, Greenwich. 7400 copies.

111. *Herbs and Herb Gardens* Jill Davies, 1983, 0 85263 656 3; cover: cp the Tudor Garden at the Tudor House Museum, Southampton. 7400 copies. Reprinted.

112. *Veteran Motor Cars* Michael E. Ware, 1983, 0 85263 658 X; cover: cp 1901 Progress and 1913 Fiat at National Motor Museum, Beaulieu. 7500 copies. Reprinted.

113. *Clogs and Clogmaking* Jeremy Atkinson, 1984, 0 85263 665 2; cover: cp author at workbench. 6600 copies.

114. *Dry Stone Walls* Lawrence Garner, 1984, 0 85263 660 0; cover: cp waller at work in the Cotswolds. 7400 copies. Reprinted.

115. *Falconry* Emma Ford, 1984, 0 85263 667 9; cover: cp author with peregrine and English pointer. 7500 copies. Reprinted.

116. *English Drinking Glasses 1675-1825* L. M. Bickerton, 1984, 0 85263 661 X; cover: cp three wine glasses *c.*1770. 7400 copies. Reprinted.

117. *Wig, Hairdressing and Shaving Bygones* Gail Durbin, 1984, 0 85263 663 6; cover: cp collection of barber and hairdressing equipment. 7500 copies.

118. *Rare Breeds* Lawrence Alderson, 1984, 0 85263 677 6; cover: cp Longhorn cattle. 7500 copies. 2nd ed, 1989, 0 7478 0002 2.

119. *Framework Knitting* Marilyn Palmer, 1984, 0 85263 668 7; cover: watercolour of hand frame worker at G. H. Hurt and Son. 5000 copies. Reprinted.

120. *Goss and Other Crested China* Nicholas J. Pine, 1984, 0 85263 662 8; cover: cp Goss model of costrel with arms of Lynmouth. 7500 copies. Reprinted.

121. *Tennis, Squash and Badminton Bygones* Gerald N. Gurney, 1984, 0 85263 676 8; cover: print of tennis match by Arthur Hopkins, 1886.

122. *Buttonhooks and Shoehorns* Sue Brandon, 1984, 0 85263 696 2; cover: cp display of hooks and horns. 7400 copies. Reprinted.

123. *Old Working Dogs* David Hancock, 1984, 0 85263 678 4; cover: print of a setter. 7400 copies.

124. *Early Electrical Appliances* Bob Gordon, 1984, 0 85263 694 6; cover: cp demonstrator with Beatty wooden tub electric washing machine. 6400 copies.

125. *Ploughs and Ploughing* Roy Brigden, 1984, 0 85263 695 4; cover: coloured engraving 'Ploughing near Scarva, County Down' *c.*1780 by William Hincks. 7400 copies.

126. *Crochet* Pauline Turner, 1984, 0 85263 697 0; cover: cp crocheting and various table accessories. 7300 copies. 2nd ed, 1990, 0 7478 0068 5.

127. *Fancy Dress* Anthea Jarvis and Patricia Raine, 1984, 0 85263 698 9; cover: hand-coloured engraving fancy dress 'The Rainbow' *c.*1868.

128. *Animal-powered Machines* J. Kenneth Major, 1985, 0 85263 710 1; cover: print donkey wheel at Broad Hinton.

129. *The Country Garage* Llyn E. Morris, 1985, 0 85263 711 X; cover: Shell advertisement 1925 by D. C. Fougueray. 7400 copies.

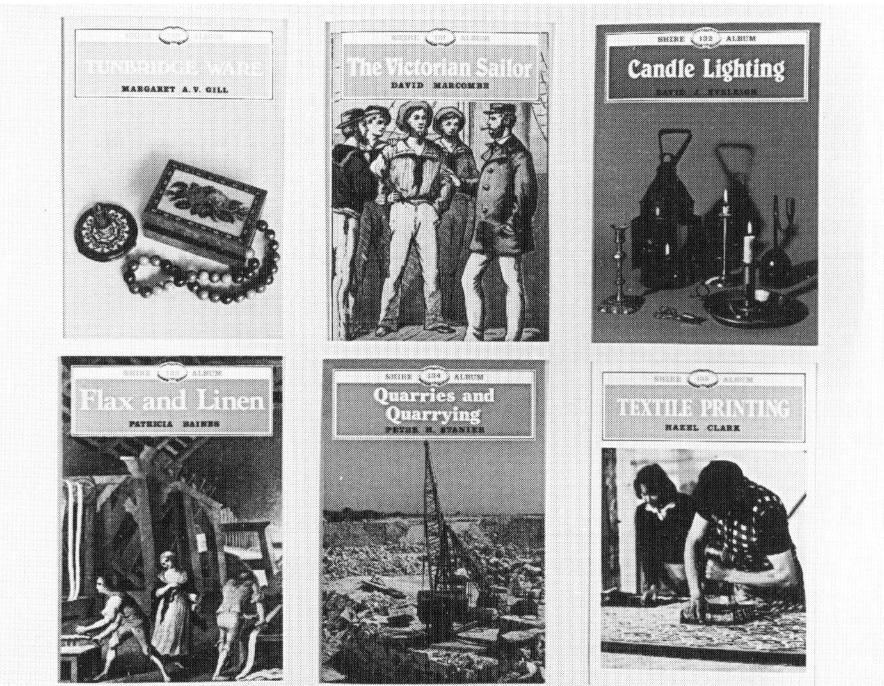

130. *Tunbridge Ware* Margaret A. V. Gill, 1985, 0 85263 712 8; cover: cp Tunbridge ware box, beads and candle-holder. 7400 copies. Reprinted.

131. *The Victorian Sailor* David Marcombe, 1985, 0 85263 713 6; cover: print of group of seamen *c*.1860. 7300 copies.

132. *Candle Lighting* David J. Eveleigh, 1985, 0 85263 726 8; cover: cp lantern and candlesticks by Ron Mason. 7300 copies. Reprinted.

133. *Flax and Linen* Patricia Baines, 1985, 0 85263 727 6; cover: coloured engraving workers in bleach mill 1783 by William Hincks. 7400 copies. Reprinted.

134. *Quarries and Quarrying* Peter Stanier, 1985, 0 85263 728 4; cover: cp Weston Quarry, Portland, by the author.

135. *Textile Printing* Hazel Clark, 1985, 0 85263 729 2; cover: cp block printer at work. 7300 copies.

136. *Billiards and Snooker Bygones* Norman Clare, 1985, 0 85263 730 6; cover: print Thurston Match Hall 1839. 7400 copies.

137. *Toy Steam Engines* Bob Gordon, 1985, 0 85263 775 6; cover: cp Doll electric-light plant 1925. 7200 copies.

138. *Old Lorries* John Woodhams, 1985, 0 85263 732 2; cover: cp Ford model AA truck 1931 by the author. 7300 copies. Reprinted.

139. *Tin and Tin Mining* R. L. Atkinson, 1985, 0 85263 733 0; cover: cp pumping engine house, Wheal Edward, by Tony Clarke. 7200 copies. Reprinted.

140. *Mauchline Ware and Associated Scottish Souvenir Ware* John Baker, 1985, 0 85263 734 9; cover: cp Mauchline ware items showing different finishes. 7300 copies. Reprinted.

141. *Old Aeroplanes* David Ogilvy, 1985, 0 85263 735 7; cover: cp Bristol F2B fighter. 7500 copies. 2nd ed, 1991, 0 7478 0107 X.

142. *Parian Ware* Dennis Barker, 1985, 0 85263 737 3; cover: cp 'Three Graces'. 7300 copies.

143. *Traction Engines* Harold Bonnett, 1985, 0 85263 738 1; cover: cp Fowler B6 class 'Super Lion' showman's engine. 7400 copies. Reprinted.

144. *Hydraulic Machines* Adrian Jarvis, 1985, 0 85263 751 9; cover: cp boat lift at Goole by the author.

145. *Industrial Narrow Gauge Railways* Ian Dean, 1985, 0 85263 752 7; cover: cp 'Wendy' saddle tank locomotive by David H. Smith. 7400 copies. Reprinted.

146. *Vintage Motor Cars* Bill Boddy, 1985, 0 85263 776 4; cover: cp 1923 Austin Seven and 1929 Bean at National Motor Museum, Beaulieu. 7200 copies. Reprinted.

147. *Old Toys* Pauline Flick, 1985, 0 85263 754 3; cover: cp two rows of dolls and other toys at Sotheby's. 7400 copies. Reprinted.

148. *Old Trams* Keith Turner, 1985, 0 85263 736 5; cover: cp Dudley, Stourbridge and District tram at Black Country Museum by the author. 7400 copies. Reprinted.

149. *Church Monuments* Brian Kemp, 1985, 0 85263 768 3; cover: cp 1621 monument of Sir Benjamin and Lady Tichborne at Tichborne, Hampshire, by Simon Eager.

150. *The London Taxi* Nick Georgano, 1985, 0 85263 772 1; cover: advertisement 1929 Morris Commercial G type international taxicab.

151. *Classic Motor Cars* Jonathan Wood, 1985, 0 85263 771 3; cover: cp 1947 Healey at National Motor Museum, Beaulieu. 7400 copies. Reprinted.

152. *The MG* F. Wilson McComb, 1985, 0 85263 773 X; cover: cp 1938 MG TA by the author. 7400 copies. Reprinted.

153. *Steam Cars* Richard J. Evans, 1985, 0 85263 774 8; cover: cp 1904 Stanley steam car.

154. *Looms and Weaving* Anna Benson and Neil Warburton, 1986, 0 85263 753 5; cover: cp weaving silk damask at Humphries Weaving Company in Essex. 7400 copies. Reprinted.

155. *Shoemaking* June Swann, 1986, 0 85263 778 0; cover: oil painting 'The Shoemaker Teaching the Linnet to Sing' by David Teniers the younger. 7300 copies.

156. *Baking and Bakeries* H. G. Muller, 1986, 0 85263 801 9; cover: oil painting 'The Baker Calls' by J. E. Berckheyde.

157. *British Sheep Breeds* Elizabeth Henson, 1986, 0 85263 779 9; cover: cp Scotch Halfbred ewes being herded, by Michael Pitts. 7500 copies. Reprinted.

158. *Canal Architecture* Peter L. Smith, 1986, 0 85263 762 4; cover: cp canalside warehouse at Shardlow. 7600 copies.

159. *Charcoal and Charcoal Burning* D. W. Kelley, 1986, 0 85263 731 4; cover: cp a charcoal burn.

160. *The Gunpowder Industry* Glenys Crocker, 1986, 0 85263 780 2; cover: cp gunpowder mortar at Powdermills.

161. *Old Telephones* Andrew Emmerson, 1986, 0 85263 781 0; cover: cp British Post Office skeleton telephone 1900. 7400 copies. Reprinted.

162. *Pressed Flint Glass* Raymond Notley, 1986, 0 85263 782 9; cover: cp a glass swan and tableware by the author.

163. *Portable Steam Engines* Lyndon R. Shearman, 1986, 0 85263 783 7; cover: cp Ransomes, Sims and Jefferies portable engine by Michael Clark. 7400 copies.

164. *Scottish Knitting* Helen Bennett, 1986, 0 85263 784 5; cover: cp model wearing Kilmarnock bonnet.

165. *Three-wheelers* Ken Hill, 1986, 0 85263 785 3; cover: cp six vehicles at National Motor Museum, Beaulieu. 7500 copies.

166. *East Anglian Village and Town Signs* Ursula Bourne, 1986, 0 85263 786 1; cover: cp village sign at Redgrave. 7200 copies.

167. *Steamboats* M. K. Stammers, 1986, 0 85263 787 X; cover: cp steamboat 'Gondola' on Coniston Water.

168. *Early Plastics* Sylvia Katz, 1986, 0 85263 790 X; cover: cp 1920-1940 plastic domestic ware. 7800 copies.

169. *Magic Lanterns* Derek Greenacre, 1986, 0 85263 791 8; cover: cp Newton mahogany magic lantern by George Skipper.

170. *Maling and other Tyneside Pottery* R. C. Bell, 1986, 0 85263 792 6; cover: cp Maling jar and jug produced for Ringtons tea merchants. 7500 copies. Reprinted.

171. *Staffordshire Figures of the Nineteenth Century* Amoret and Christopher Scott, 1986, 0 85263 793 4; cover: cp figure of Florence Nightingale with a wounded soldier. 7400 copies.

172. *First World War Tanks* E. Bartholomew, 1986, 0 85263 799 3; cover: cp Tank Museum's Mark V (male), 1918.

173. *Early Bicycles* Nick Clayton, 1986, 0 85263 803 5; cover: fashion plate of family on tricycles. 7400 copies. Reprinted.

174. *The Safety Bicycle* Ian Jones, 1986, 0 85263 804 3; cover: cp selection of bicycles at Mark Hall Cycle Museum.

175. *Balloons and Ballooning* John A. Baker and Norman Pritchard, 1986, 0 85263 805 1; cover: cp aerial view of Bristol Balloon Fiesta by I. Culley.

176. *Sundials* Christopher St J. H. Daniel, 1986, 0 85263 808 6; cover: cp dolphin sundial at National Maritime Museum by the author. 7400 copies. Reprinted.

177. *Old Cooking Utensils* David J. Eveleigh, 1986, 0 85263 812 4; cover: watercolour kitchen scene by William Locke. 7200 copies. Reprinted.

178. *Children's Cars* Paul Pennell, 1986, 0 85263 833 7; cover: cp 1920 Peerless pedal car by the author.

179. *Delftware Tiles* Hans van Lemmen, 1986, 0 85263 834 5; cover: cp panel of Dutch delftware tiles. 7200 copies.

180. *Drawing Instruments 1850-1950* Michael Scott-Scott, 1986, 0 85263 835 3; cover: cp 1889 mahogany case of instruments.

181. *Motor Scooters* Michael Webster, 1986, 0 85263 836 1; cover: cp 1958 Vespa and 1962 Lambretta by the author. 7500 copies.

182. *Victorian Souvenir Medals* Daniel Fearon, 1986, 0 85263 837 X; cover: cp collector's cabinet and medals.

183. *Austerity Motoring 1939-1950* Andrew Lane, 1987, 0 85263 841 8; cover: cp 1938 8 hp Morris in wartime trim.

184. *Church Tiles of the Nineteenth Century* Kenneth Beaulah, 1987, 0 85263 842 6; cover: cp panel of tiles from reredos of Christ Church, Scarborough.

185. *Early Vehicle Lighting* Peter W. Card, 1987, 0 85263 843 4; cover: 1924 Powell and Hammer catalogue cover.

186. *Naval Cannon* John Munday, 1987, 0 85263 844 2; cover: oil painting 'Nelson Falling' by Denis Dighton.

187. *Old Delivery Vans* Nick Baldwin, 1987, 0 85263 845 0; cover: magazine illustration of 1933 Bedford 2 ton boarded tilt van. 7500 copies.

188. *Old Letter Boxes* Martin Robinson, 1987, 0 85263 846 9; cover: cp early pillar box at Barnes Cross, near Sherborne, by the author. 7500 copies.

189. *Scottish Coins* Donald Bateson, 1987, 0 85263 847 7; cover: cp 1603 gold sword and sceptre piece of James VI.

190. *Scottish Doocots* Tim Buxbaum, 1987, 0 85263 848 5; cover: cp Johnstounburn doocot.

191. *Scottish Pottery* Graeme Cruickshank, 1987, 0 85263 849 3; cover: cp jug by J. and M. P. Bell of Glasgow.

192. *Sports Cars* Ian Dussek, 1987, 0 85263 850 7; cover: cp 1934 Bugatti Type 57.

193. *Toy Boats* Basil Harley, 1987, 0 85263 851 5; cover: cp 1909 Marklin 'Lusitania' by the author.

194. *The Silk Industry* Sarah Bush, 1987, 0 85263 706 3; cover: watercolour gathering mulberry leaves by Grahame Tomkins. 7500 copies. Reprinted.

195. *The Cutlery Industry* Peter Smithurst, 1987, 0 85263 870 1; cover: oil painting *c.*1860 'The Two Grinders' by Godfrey Sykes.

196. *The Jaguar* Andrew Whyte, 1987, 0 85263 871 X; cover: cp 1951 Jaguar Mark Seven and 1987 Jaguar XJ6 by the author. 7500 copies. Reprinted.

197. *Motoring Costume* Andrew Lane, 1987, 0 85263 872 8; cover: advertisement for Humber cars *c.*1910.

198. *The Rolls-Royce* Jonathan Wood, 1987, 0 85263 873 6; cover: cp 1911 Silver Ghost.

199. *Old Docks* Nancy Ritchie-Noakes, 1987, 0 85263 893 0; cover: cp Albert Dock, Liverpool, by the author.

200. *Historic Ships* M. K. Stammers, 1987, 0 85263 894 9; cover: cp RRS 'Discovery' and figurehead of HMS 'Unicorn' in Victoria Dock, Dundee.

201. *Copper and Copper Mining* R. L. Atkinson, 1987, 0 85263 895 7; cover: cp molten copper being poured.

202. *London Street Markets* Debra Shipley and Mary Peplow, 1987, 0 85263 899 X; cover: print 'The Gingerbread Man' from 'Cries of London' by F. Wheatley.

203. *London Theatres and Concert Halls* Debra Shipley and Mary Peplow, 1987, 0 85263 900 7; cover: coloured engraving interior of Drury Lane Theatre.

204. *Bee Boles and Bee Houses* A. M. Foster, 1988, 0 85263 903 1; cover: cp Victorian bee house at Berkshire College of Agriculture by the author.

205. *Gentlemen's Dress Accessories* E. Eckstein, J. and G. Firkins, 1987, 0 85263 904 X; cover: cp display of accessories by Michael Pugsley.

206. *Church Memorial Brasses and Brass Rubbing* Leigh Chapman, 1987, 0 85263 905 8; cover: cp brass rubbers at Cirencester parish church.

207. *Model Steam Engines* Bob Gordon, 1987, 0 85263 906 6; cover: cp model Savage engine built by Mrs Cherry Hill, photograph by Mike Wade.

208. *Picture Postcards* C. W. Hill, 1987, 0 85263 907 4; cover: cp selection of picture postcards. 7600 copies. Reprinted

209. *Early Armoured Cars* E. Bartholomew, 1988, 0 85263 908 2; cover: cp 1920 Rolls-Royce armoured car.

210. *Scent Bottles* Alexandra Walker, 1987, 0 85263 909 0; cover: cp group of scent bottles. 7400 copies. Reprinted.

211. *Spoons 1650-1930* Simon Moore, 1987, 0 85263 910 4; cover: cp fan of silver and gilt spoons by the author. 7600 copies. Reprinted.

212. *Bellfounding* Trevor S. Jennings, 1988, 0 85263 911 2; cover: cp casting a bell by the author.

213. *Dovecotes* Peter and Jean Hansell, 1988, 0 85263 920 1; cover: cp dovecote at Notley Abbey by the authors.

214. *Dummy Boards and Chimney Boards* Clare Graham, 1988, 0 85263 921 X; cover: cp dummy board 'Vanity'.

215. *Old Trolleybuses* David Kaye, 1988, 0 85263 922 8; cover: cp Sunbeam S7 trolley-bus.

216. *Optical Toys* Basil Harley, 1988, 0 85263 923 6; cover: cp Emile Reynaud's Praxinoscope Theatre 1877.

217. *Playing-cards and Tarots* George Beal, 1988, 0 85263 924 4; cover: cp six cards by the author.

218. *Scottish Agricultural Implements* Bob Powell, 1988, 0 85263 925 2; cover: cp R. G. Garvie and Sons portable threshing mill.

219. *Triumph Sports Cars* Graham Robson, 1988, 0 85263 926 0; cover: cp 1970 Triumph GT6 coupé by Micro Decet.

220. *Barometers* Anita McConnell, 1988, 0 85263 963 5; cover: cp Watkins and Smith diagonal barometer 1763 by Michael Bass.

221. *Four-wheel Drive and Land-Rover* Nick Baldwin, 1988, 0 85263 964 3; cover: cp 1948 Land-Rover.

222. *Old Sheffield Plate* Anneke Bambery, 1988, 0 85263 965 1; cover: cp 1815 Old Sheffield Plate inkstand.

223. *Penknives and other Folding Knives* Simon Moore, 1988, 0 85263 966 X; cover: cp arrangement of knives by the author.

224. *Pomanders, Posies and Pot-pourri* Jessica Houdret, 1988, 0 85263 967 8; cover: cp pot-pourris, pomanders, sachets and posies by the author. 7200 copies. Reprinted.

225. *Teddy Bears and Soft Toys* Pauline Cockrill, 1988, 0 85263 968 6; cover: cp bears and Mickey Mouse by Pip Barnard. 7500 copies. Reprinted.

226. *The Volkswagen Beetle* Jonathan Wood, 1989, 0 85263 974 0; cover: cp 1953 Beetle Export G model.

227. *Spectacles, Lorgnettes and Monocles* D. C. Davidson, 1989, 0 85263 975 9; cover: cp various spectacles and cases.

228. *The Aston Martin* Alan Archer, 1989, 0 85263 980 5; cover: cp 1961 Aston Martin DB4 by Fred Stevens.

229. *Dyeing and Dyestuffs* Su Grierson, 1989, 0 85263 978 3; cover: cp dyestuffs and dyed fabrics.

230. *Church Misericords and Bench Ends* Richard Hayman, 1989, 0 85263 996 1; cover: cp choir stalls at Beverley Minster by the author.

231. *Royal Dockyards* Philip Macdougall, 1989, 0 7478 0032 2; cover: coloured engraving 1853 Portsmouth dockyard.

232. *Firefighting Equipment* Brian Wright, 1989, 0 7478 0034 0; cover: lithograph 1825 'London Fire Engines'.

233. *Golfing Bygones* Dale Concannon, 1989, 0 7478 0035 9; cover: oil painting 1894 'The Bunker' by Charles Edmund Brock.

234. *Harvesting Machinery* Roy Brigden, 1989, 0 85263 979 1; cover: cp 1956 Massey Ferguson combine harvester.

235. *Industrial Steam Locomotives* Geoffrey Hayes, 1989, 0 7478 0036 7; cover: cp 1914 0-4-2ST steam locomotive Prestongrange number 7 by the author.

236. *Limekilns and Limeburning* Richard Williams, 1989, 0 7478 0037 5; cover: cp Beadnell limekilns.

237. *Motor Cars of the 1930s* Ian Dussek, 1989, 0 85263 981 3; cover: cp Rolls Bentley 3½ litre sports saloon.

238. *The Scottish Motor Industry* Michael Worthington-Williams, 1989, 0 7478 0038 3; cover: catalogue illustration 1925 Arrol-Johnston tourer.

239. *Tugs and Towage* M. K. Stammers, 1989, 0 7478 0039 1; cover: print 1930 steamtug and liner at Liverpool by Sam Brown.

240. *Funicular Railways* John Woodhams, 1989, 0 7478 0040 5; cover: cp East Hill Lift at Hastings by the author.

241. *Handbells* Trevor S. Jennings, 1989, 0 7478 0044 8; cover: cp various handbells by the author.

242. *Tiled Furniture* Hans van Lemmen, 1989, 0 7478 0046 4; cover: cp mahogany wash-stand with Maw tiles *c.*1875 by Richard Bishop.

243. *Fans* Hélène Alexander, 1989, 0 7478 0045 6; cover: cp two silk fans painted by Billotey.

244. *The Humber* Nick Georgano, 1990, 0 7478 0057 X; cover: cp 1907 Coventry Humber 15 hp tourer.

245. *Staff Cars* David Fletcher, 1990, 0 7478 0058 8; cover: cp Vauxhall D type staff car *c.*1918.

246. *Embroidered Stuart Pictures* Margaret Swain, 1990, 0 7478 0059 6; cover: cp the Rous-Lench casket.

247. *Calculating Machines and Computers* Geoffrey Tweedale, 1990, 0 7478 0080 4; cover: cp Napier's 'bones', abacus, slide-rule and calculator.

248. *Constructional Toys* Basil Harley, 1990, 0 7478 0081 2; cover: cp Meccano windmill.

249. *Decorative Leadwork* P. M. Sutton-Goold, 1990, 0 7478 0082 0; cover: cp leaden cistern at Neston Park by Jonathan Gaunt.

250. *Cast Iron* Jacqueline Fearn, 1990, 0 7478 0083 9; cover: cp the Maharajah's Well, Stoke Row.

251. *The Brighton Run* Lord Montagu of Beaulieu, 1990, 0 7478 0099 5; cover: cp 1903 Humberette at start of Brighton Run by Michael Bass.

252. *The Flute* Jeremy Montagu, 1990, 0 7478 0085 5; cover: cp flautist playing silver flute made by Eugène Albert, by Michael Bass.

253. *Four-poster and Tester Beds* Ivan G. Sparkes, 1990, 0 7478 0078 2; cover: cp four-poster bed at Scone Palace.

254. *The French Horn* Jeremy Montagu, 1990, 0 7478 0086 3; cover: cp horn player playing a hand horn, by Michael Bass.

255. *Toy Trains* David Salisbury, 1990, 0 7478 0087 1; cover: cp Hornby Gauge 0 layout.

256. *Walking Sticks* Catherine Dike, 1990, 0 7478 0079 0; cover: cp assortment of canes by the author.

257. *London Inn Signs* Dominic Rotheroe, 1990, 0 7478 0088 X; cover: cp Rising Sun Inn, Cloth Fair, London.

258. *Snuff* Ursula Bourne, 1990, 0 7478 0089 8; cover: watercolour eighteenth-century fop by Rachel Lewis.

259. *Airships* Patrick Abbott, 1991, 0 7478 0084 7; cover: cp Skyship 500 over Manhattan.

260. *Old Gramophones and other Talking Machines* Benet Bergonzi, 1991, 0 7478 0104 5; cover: cp 1906 Pathéphone Modèle F with 'Morning Glory' horn.

261. *Stables and Stable Blocks* Christopher Powell, 1991, 0 7478 0105 3; cover: cp stables at Moccas Court.

262. *The Victorian Farmer* David J. Eveleigh, 1991, 0 7478 0106 1; cover: oil painting 1856 farmer and prize Shorthorn by William Smith.

263. *The Land Speed Record* David Tremayne, 1991, 0 7478 0115 0; cover: cp Richard Noble's Thrust 2 in Nevada in 1983.

264. *Mazes* Adrian Fisher and Diana Kingham, 1991, 0 7478 0116 9; cover: cp maze at Hever Castle.

265. *Motor-car Mascots and Badges* Peter W. Card, 1991, 0 7478 0117 7; cover: cp group of mascots and badges at National Motor Museum, Beaulieu.

266. *Motoring Specials* Ian Dussek, 1991, 0 7478 0118 5; cover: cp John Bolster's 'Bloody Mary' at National Motor Museum, Beaulieu.

267. *Touring Caravans* Jon Pressnell, 1991, 0 7478 0119 3; cover: cp 1928 Eccles de luxe caravan by Paul Shinton.

268. *The Slate Industry* Merfyn Williams, 1991, 0 7478 0124 X; cover: cp Llechwedd slate quarry.

269. *Soft Drinks* Colin Emmins, 1991, 0 7478 0125 8; cover: print lemonade stall *c*.1835.

270. *Police Uniform and Equipment* A. A. Clarke, 1991, 0 7478 0126 6; cover: oil painting *c*.1840 constable of Kingston upon Hull.

271. *Dolls' Houses* Halina Pasierbska, 1991, 0 7478 0135 5; cover: cp Tate Baby House 1760.

272. *Early Electric Trains* R. L. Vickers, 1991, 0 7478 0136 3; cover: cp Liverpool Overhead Railway train 1956 by T. J. Edgington.

273. *Firemen's Uniform* Brian Wright, 1991, 0 7478 0137 1; cover: cp two firemen, one in modern uniform, the other in 1810 uniform of Norwich Union Insurance Company.

274. *Rocking Horses* Ruth Bottomley, 1991, 0 7478 0138 X; cover: cp dappled grey English rocking horse 1880 by Andy White.

275. *Table Settings* Robin Emmerson, 1991, 0 7478 0139 8; cover: cp pyramid of glass salvers, some containing 'ribbon jelly'.

276. *Wallpaper* Clare Taylor, 1991, 0 7478 0140 1; cover: painting *c*.1842 wallpaper manufactory.

History in Camera

Conceived in 1972 as a vehicle for hitherto little published period photographs, at that time underused as historic source material, the series was overtaken by the boom in picture books of old photographs and was extended only occasionally. Each title comprises a text of 8000 to 10,000 words and about 100 photographs with lengthy captions. The books are A5 format (210 mm by 150 mm), square-backed with spines, and of varying extent. They were not originally numbered within the series.

1. *East Coast Shipping* A. A. C. Hedges, 1974, 0 85263 259 9 (hardbacked), 0 85263 251 7 (paperbacked), 96pp; cover: photo seaman at wheel with trawler inset in wheel, design by Ron Shaddock, blue yellow and black. Hardback 1000 copies, paperback 2800 copies. 2nd ed (paperback only), 1989, 0 85263 999 6; new cover: cp steam drifter *Lydia Eva* on river Yare by Brian Ollington. Verso erroneously carries ISBNs of previous edition.

2. *Victoria's Wars* I. F. W. Beckett, 1974, 0 85263 258 4, 88pp; cover: photo Maxim-gun detachment 1895, design by Ron Shaddock, brown purple and black. 3000 copies. Reprinted.

3. *Farming with Steam* Harold Bonnett, 1974, 0 85263 285 1, 88pp; cover: photos corn binder 1907 and portable engine threshing oats 1912, design by Ron Shaddock, green olive and black. 2800 copies. Reprinted.

4. *West Coast Shipping* M. K. Stammers, 1976, 0 85263 361 0, 88pp; cover: photo brig under full sail, design by Ron Shaddock, blues and black. 2600 copies. 2nd ed, 1983, 0 85263 642 3; cover change: light blue omitted. 1989, new cover: cp Isle of Man steamer.

5. *British Railways' Steam Locomotives* F. G. Cockman, 1980, 0 85263 531 1, 80pp; cover: cp locomotive 'The Middlesex Regiment' near Ampthill by the author. 4700 copies. 2nd ed, 1990, 0 7478 0070 7.

6. *Hops and Hop Picking* Richard Filmer, 1982, 0 85263 617 2, 80pp; cover: print families picking hops. 4800 copies. Reprinted.

7. *Wedding Fashions 1860-1980* Avril Lansdell, 1983, 0 85263 624 5, 112pp; cover: cp 1910 wedding couple in gold oval frame on blue ground. 4800 copies. 2nd ed, 1986, 0 85263 839 6.

8. *Fashion à la Carte 1860-1900* Avril Lansdell, 1985, 0 85263 747 0, 96pp; cover: cp 1860s carte in decorative frame on red ground. 4900 copies.

9. *Canals and Waterways* Michael E. Ware, 1987, 0 85263 878 7, 88pp; cover: coloured postcard 1905 Widcombe flight of locks in Bath. 4800 copies. Reprinted.

10. *Seaside Fashions 1860-1939* Avril Lansdell, 1990, 0 7478 0066 9; cover: cp 1908 bathers in shell frame on beige ground.

SHIRE ARCHAEOLOGY

The Shire Archaeology series was originally suggested by David Hinton and began in 1974 under the series editorship of James Dyer. The books are A5 format (210 mm by 150mm) and square-backed with a spine but of variable extent, from 48 to 96 pages. The cover design by Ron Shaddock has remained unchanged, with typefaces for series, title and author uniform for each book, and allows for a full colour rectangular photograph below the type, all on a white ground. The illustration was repeated on the back cover of early editions of numbers 1 to 18, 20 and 21. Subsequently it was replaced on the back cover with text. The series number appears on the spine of all but the first editions of numbers 1 to 11 and the second edition of number 3. Number 12 was the first to be given a series number and numbers were then allotted retrospectively to previous titles. There is no reference to the series number on the verso. The first title, *Anglo-Saxon Jewellery*, was published simultaneously in hard cover with a dust jacket and in paperback.

1. *Anglo-Saxon Jewellery* Ronald Jessup, 1974, 0 85263 261 4 (hardback), 0 85263 262 2 (paperback), 96pp; cover: cp the Alfred Jewel. 1000 copies (hardback), 1900 copies (paperback).

2. *Flint Implements of the Old Stone Age* Peter Timms, 1974, 0 85263 264 9, 56pp; cover: hand axe on red ground. 3300 copies. The verso refers to the paperback edition but there was no other. 2nd ed, 1980, 0 85263 517 6; new cover: cp hand axe on green ground.

3. *Pottery in Roman Britain* Vivien G. Swan, 1975, 0 85263 268 1, 56pp; cover: cp New Forest painted flagon. 4100 copies. 2nd ed, 1978, 0 85263 425 0, 64pp. 3rd ed, 1980, 0 85263 525 7. 4th ed, 1988, 0 85263 912 0, 80pp.

4. *Bronze Age Metalwork in England and Wales* Nancy G. Langmaid, 1976, 0 85263 266 5, 64pp; cover: cp replica of early bronze age dagger. 2800 copies. The title *Bronze Age Metalwork in Southern Britain*, no. 39, is a completely different book.

5. *Anglo-Saxon Pottery* David H. Kennett, 1978, 0 85263 424 2, 56pp; cover: cp fifth-century Buckelurne. 4100 copies. 2nd ed, 1989, 0 7478 0006 5, 68pp.

6. *Medieval Pottery* Jeremy Haslam, 1978, 0 85263 438 2, 64pp; cover: cp fourteenth-century jug. 4000 copies. 2nd ed, 1984, 0 85263 670 9, 64pp.

7. *Prehistoric Pottery* Nancy G. Langmaid, 1978, 0 85263 423 4, 64pp; cover: cp Dorchester-on-Thames beaker. 4100 copies.

8. *Barrows in England and Wales* Leslie V. Grinsell, 1979, 0 85263 461 7, 64pp; cover: cp Arthur's Stone, Dorstone. 4800 copies. 2nd ed, 1984, 0 85263 669 5. 3rd ed, 1990, 0 7478 0052 9.

9. *Prehistoric Stone Circles* Aubrey Burl, 1979, 0 85263 457 9, 48pp; cover: cp Swinside Stone Circle, Cumbria. 5000 copies. 2nd ed, 1983, 0 85263 640 7. 3rd ed, 1988, 0 85263 962 7, 56pp.

10. *Roman Roads* Richard W. Bagshawe, 1979, 0 85263 458 7, 64pp; cover: cp Roman road between Wroxeter and Leintwardine. 4900 copies. Reprinted.

11. *Roman Villas* David E. Johnston, 1979, 0 85263 459 5, 64pp; cover: cp model of villa at Sparsholt, Hampshire. 4900 copies. 2nd ed, 1983, 0 85263 641 5. 3rd ed, 1988, 0 85263 961 9.

12. *Roman Coinage in Britain* P. J. Casey, 1980, 0 85263 494 3, 64pp; cover: cp coin of Emperor Claudius. 4800 copies. 2nd ed, 1984, 0 85263 671 7.

13. *Towns in Roman Britain* Julian Bennett, 1980, 0 85263 495 1, 72pp; cover: cp Roman theatre at Verulamium. 4800 copies. 2nd ed, 1984, 0 85263 672 5.

14. *Later Stone Implements* Michael Pitts, 1980, 0 85263 518 4, 56pp; cover: cp arrowheads from Scotland. 4700 copies.

15. *Ancient Agricultural Implements* Sian Rees, 1981, 0 85263 535 4, 72pp; cover: cp Piercebridge bronze of ploughman and team. 4700 copies.

16. *Hillforts of England and Wales* James Dyer, 1981, 0 85263 536 2, 64pp; cover: cp Hambledon Hillfort. 4800 copies. Reprinted.

17. *Wood in Archaeology* Maisie Taylor, 1981, 0 85263 537 0, 56pp; cover: cp pinewood figure from Roos Carr. 4600 copies.

18. *Anglo-Saxon Architecture* Mary and Nigel Kerr, 1983, 0 85263 570 2, 72pp; cover: cp Earls Barton church tower. 4700 copies. Reprinted.

19. *Roman Military Tombstones* Alastair Scott Anderson, 1984, 0 85263 571 0, 64pp; cover: cp tombstone of Sextus Valerius Genialis.

20. *Fengate* Francis Pryor, 1982, 0 85263 577 X; 56pp; cover: cp ring-ditch at Fengate.

21. *Medieval Jewellery* David Hinton, 1982, 0 85263 576 1, 48pp, cover: cp the Thame ring. 4600 copies.

22. *Aerial Archaeology in Britain* D. N. Riley, 1982, 0 85263 592 3, 56pp; cover: cp three ring ditches at Clanfield, Oxfordshire. 4900 copies. Reprinted.

23. *Deserted Villages* Trevor Rowley and John Wood, 1982, 0 85263 593 1, 72pp; cover: cp deserted village site near Aston Abbotts, Buckinghamshire. 5000 copies. Reprinted.

24. *Roman Crafts and Industries* Alan McWhirr, 1982, 0 85263 594 X, 64pp; cover: cp mosaicist's workshop at Corinium Museum. 4900 copies. Reprinted.

25. *Romano-British Mosaics* Peter Johnson, 1982, 0 85263 616 4, 64pp; cover: cp Orpheus mosaic at Littlecote Park. 4900 copies. 2nd ed, 1987, 0 85263 891 4, 72pp.

26. *Medieval Roads* Brian Paul Hindle, 1982, 0 85263 600 8, 64pp; cover: Gough map. 4800 copies. 2nd ed, 1989, 0 85263 997 X.

Shire Archaeology
Anglo-Saxon Jewellery
Shire Archaeology
Flint Implements of the Old Stone Age
Shire Archaeology
Pottery in Roman Britain
Shire Archaeology
Bronze Age Metalwork in England and Wales
Shire Archaeology
Anglo-Saxon Pottery
Shire Archaeology
Medieval Pottery
Shire Archaeology
Prehistoric Pottery
Shire Archaeology
Barrows in England and Wales
Shire Archaeology
Prehistoric Stone Circles
Shire Archaeology
Roman Roads
Shire Archaeology
Roman Villas
Shire Archaeology
Roman Coinage in Britain
Shire Archaeology
Towns in Roman Britain
Shire Archaeology
Later Stone Implements
Shire Archaeology
Ancient Agricultural Implements
Shire Archaeology
Hillforts of England and Wales

27. *Village Plans* Brian K. Roberts, 1982, 0 85263 601 6; 56pp; cover: cp Tunstall, near Sunderland. 4600 copies.

28. *Medieval Fields* David Hall, 1982, 0 85263 599 0, 56pp; cover: cp ridge and furrow at Naseby. 4800 copies. Reprinted.

29. *Teaching Archaeology in Schools* James Dyer, 1983, 0 85263 622 9, 64pp; cover: cp school party at Hadrian's Wall.

30. *The Archaeology of Gardens* Christopher Taylor, 1983, 0 85263 625 3, 72pp; cover: cp garden remains at Holdenby, Northamptonshire. 4900 copies. Reprinted.

31. *Ancient Boats* Sean McGrail, 1983, 0 85263 626 1, 64pp; cover: cp gold model boat from Broighter, Co. Derry. 5100 copies.

32. *Prehistoric Astronomy and Ritual* Aubrey Burl, 1983, 0 85263 621 0, 56pp; cover: cp Stonehenge. 4900 copies. Reprinted.

33. *Animal Remains in Archaeology* Rosemary-Margaret Luff, 1984, 0 85263 633 4, 64pp; cover: cp cat skull.

34. *The Gods of Roman Britain* Miranda J. Green, 1983, 0 85263 634 2, 76pp; cover: cp *Deae Matres* relief, Cirencester. 5000 copies. Reprinted.

35. *Greek Coinage* N. K. Rutter, 1983, 0 85263 635 0, 56pp; cover: cp a tetradrachm of Katane.

36. *Castles* R. Allen Brown, 1985, 0 85263 653 9; 56pp; cover: cp Raglan Castle. 4900 copies. Reprinted.

37. *Roman Forts in Britain* David J. Breeze, 1983, 0 85263 654 7, 72pp; cover: cp reconstructed gate at the Lunt fort, Baginton. 4900 copies. Reprinted.

38. *Early Celtic Art in Britain and Ireland* Ruth and Vincent Megaw, 1986, 0 85263 679 2, 64pp; cover: cp horse harness mount. 3700 copies. Reprinted.

39. *Bronze Age Metalwork in Southern Britain* Susan M. Pearce, 1984, 0 85263 680 6, 64pp; cover: cp gold ornament from Yeovil.

40. *Post-Medieval Pottery 1650-1800* Jo Draper, 1984, 0 85263 681 4, 64pp; cover: cp two earthenware coffee-pots.

41. *Celtic Warriors* W. F. and J. N. G. Ritchie, 1985, 0 85263 714 4, 56pp; cover: cp modern representation of a mounted Celtic warrior. 4900 copies. 1990; new cover: cp figure of Celtic warrior at Museum of the Iron Age, Andover.

42. *Romano-British Wall Painting* Roger Ling, 1985, 0 85263 715 2, 64pp; cover: gladiator on wall decoration from Colchester.

43. *Neolithic and Early Bronze Age Pottery* Alex Gibson, 1986, 0 85263 755 1, 64pp; cover: cp food vessel urn from Ryton.

44. *Moated Sites* David Wilson, 1985, 0 85263 756 X, 64pp; cover: cp Little Moreton Hall.

45. *Early Medieval Towns in Britain* Jeremy Haslam, 1985, 0 85263 758 6, 64pp; cover: cp Ludlow. 5000 copies.

46. *Human Bones in Archaeology* Ann Stirland, 1986, 0 85263 759 4, 64pp; cover: cp skeletons of pregnant woman and foetus. 4000 copies.

47. *Rock Carvings of Northern Britain* Stan Beckensall, 1986, 0 85263 760 8, 64pp; cover: cp rock carving at Old Bewick.

48. *Later Celtic Art in Britain and Ireland* Lloyd Laing, 1987, 0 85263 874 4, 56pp; cover: cp one of the terminals of the Tara brooch.

49. *Villages in Roman Britain* Robin Hanley, 1987, 0 85263 875 2, 64pp; cover: cp village site of Little Down.

50. *Ancient Farming* Peter J. Reynolds, 1987, 0 85263 876 0, 64pp; cover: cp research fields at Butser Ancient Farm. 4900 copies.

51. *Computer Archaeology* Gary Lock and John Wilcock, 1987, 0 85263 877 9, 64pp; cover: cp computer and potsherds.

52. *Anglo-Saxon Sculpture* James Lang, 1988, 0 85263 927 9, 60pp; cover: the Irton cross.

53. *Brochs of Scotland* J. N. G. Ritchie, 1988, 0 85263 928 7, 56pp; cover: cp the Broch of Mousa.

54. *Life in the Ice Age* Anthony J. Stuart, 1988, 0 85263 929 5, 64pp; cover: painting of mammoths by N. Arbor.

55. *Samian Ware* Guy de la Bédoyère, 1988, 0 85263 930 9, 68pp; cover: cp fragment of Dragendorff 37 bowl.

56. *Textiles in Archaeology* John Peter Wild, 1988, 0 85263 931 7, 68pp; cover: cp fragment of Roman wool tapestry.

57. *Celtic Crosses of Britain and Ireland* Malcolm Seaborne, 1989, 0 7478 0003 0, 64pp; cover: cp Cross of Muiredach.

58. *Later Prehistoric Pottery in England and Wales* Sheila M. Elsdon, 1989, 0 7478 0004 9, 68pp; cover: cp decorated jar from Dragonby.

59. *Roman Military Equipment* M. C. Bishop and J. C. Coulston, 1989, 0 7478 0005 7, 76pp; cover: cp helmet cheek-piece from South Shields.

60. *Viking Age Archaeology in Britain and Ireland* Richard Hall, 1990, 0 7478 0063 4, 64pp; cover: cp boat grave at Westness.

61. *Causewayed Enclosures* R. J. Mercer, 1990, 0 7478 0064 2, 72pp; cover: cp Windmill Hill causewayed enclosure.

62. *Medieval Town Plans* Brian Paul Hindle, 1990, 0 7478 0065 0, 64pp; cover: cp Elm Hill, Norwich.

63. *Irish Megalithic Tombs* Elizabeth Shee Twohig, 1990, 0 7478 0094 4, 72pp; cover: cp portal tomb on the Burren at Poulnabrone.

64. *Cave Art* Andrew J. Lawson, 1991, 0 7478 0120 7, 64pp; cover: painted bison at Altamira, Spain.

65. *Mesolithic Britain* John Wymer, 1991, 0 7478 0121 5, 64pp; cover: painting of mesolithic hunting scene by Tim Taylor.

66. *Prehistoric Henges* Aubrey Burl, 1991, 0 7478 0123 1, 56pp; cover: cp Giant's Ring, Ballynahatty, Co Down.

67. *Prehistoric Flint Mines* Robin Holgate, 1991, 0 7478 0141 X, 56pp; cover: cp gallery at Grimes Graves, Norfolk.

SHIRE COUNTY GUIDES

The first Shire books were guides to counties. Almost all English counties were covered in the 'Discovering' series. In 1982 a new title on Somerset was published in larger format. The success of this led to the rapid development of the Shire County Guide list, all A5 (210 mm by 150 mm), square-backed with spine and with colour photograph on the cover. The series number appears on the spine and verso. New editions are usually 'flashed' in the top right corner of the cover.

1. *Somerset* Martyn Brown, 1982, 0 85263 618 0, 56pp; cover: cp Cheddar Gorge. 4600 copies. No series number. 2nd ed, 1988, 0 85263 960 0, 68pp; new cover: cp pond at East Quantoxhead.

2. *Lincolnshire and South Humberside* David Kaye, 1984, 0 85263 682 2, 64pp; cover: cp Lincoln Cathedral. 4700 copies. 2nd ed, 1989, 0 85263 988 0.

3. *North Yorkshire and North Humberside* Cyril Bainbridge, 1984, 0 85263 683 0, 64pp; cover: cp Gordale Scar. 4700 copies. 2nd ed, 1989, 0 85263 987 2.

4. *Sussex* David J. Allen, 1984, 0 85263 684 9, 64pp; cover: cp Rottingdean. 4800 copies. 2nd ed, 1987, 0 85263 882 5. Not flashed.

5. *Wiltshire* Mark Child, 1984, 0 85263 685 7, 56pp; cover: cp Silbury Hill by Dick Walker. 4800 copies. 2nd ed, 1987, 0 85263 883 3. Not flashed.

6. *Derbyshire and the Peak District* John Anthony, 1985, 0 85263 739 X, 56pp; cover: cp Derwent Valley from Millstone Edge. 4900 copies. 2nd ed, 1990, 0 7478 0048 0.

7. *Shropshire* Lawrence Garner, 1985, 0 85263 740 3, 56pp; cover: cp Ludlow. 4900 copies. 2nd ed, 1989, 0 85263 989 9.

8. *Surrey* John Drewett, 1985, 0 85263 741 1, 64pp; cover: cp Winkworth Arboretum. 4800 copies. 2nd ed, 1990, 0 7478 0051 0.

9. *Dorset* Peter Stanier, 1986, 0 85263 806 X, 64pp; cover; cp Gold Hill, Shaftesbury. 4900 copies. 2nd ed, 1990, 0 7478 0049 9, 68pp.

10. *Essex* Stan Jarvis, 1986, 0 85263 807 8, 64pp; cover: cp Audley End House. 4900 copies. 2nd ed, 1990, 0 7478 0050 2.

11. *Staffordshire* Peter Heaton, 1986, 0 85263 809 4, 56pp; cover: cp Shugborough. 4900 copies. 2nd ed, 1991, 0 7478 0113 4.

12. *Bedfordshire* James Dyer, 1987, 0 85263 858 2, 64pp; cover: cp Silsoe by the author.

13. *Buckinghamshire* Ian F. W. Beckett, 1987, 0 85263 859 0, 56pp; cover: cp Lacey Green windmill.

14. *Cornwall* Peter Stanier, 1987, 0 85263 860 4, 64pp; cover: cp the harbour at Mullion Cove by the author.

15. *Gwent* Anna Tucker, 1987, 0 85263 861 2, 64pp; cover: cp Monnow Bridge, Monmouth, by Paul Blyton.

16. *Herefordshire and the Black Mountains* Barry Freeman, 1987, 0 85263 862 0, 56pp; cover: cp Eardisland by Kathleen Freeman. 4900 copies. 2nd ed, 1990, 0 7478 0071 5. Not flashed.

17. *Cheshire* David Packer, 1988, 0 85263 932 5, 72pp; cover: cp Sweetbriar Hall, Nantwich, by the author.

18. *Hertfordshire* Arthur Jones, 1988, 0 85263 933 3, 72pp; cover: cp Benington Lordship.

19. *Kent* John E. Vigar, 1988, 0 85263 934 1, 64pp; cover: cp Aylesford. 4800 copies. 2nd ed, 1991, 0 7478 0112 6.

20. *Oxfordshire and Oxford* Marilyn Yurdan, 1988, 0 85263 935 X, 80pp; cover: cp the Thames at Abingdon.

21. *West Yorkshire* Colin Speakman, 1988, 0 85263 936 8, 56pp; cover: cp Cloth Hall Tower at Ravensknowle Park, Huddersfield.

22. *Northamptonshire* Jack Gould, 1988, 0 85263 937 6, 68pp; cover: cp Great Weldon.

23. *Cambridgeshire and Cambridge* Ronald Russell, 1988, 0 85263 954 6, 72pp; cover: cp Ely Cathedral by the author.

24. *Hampshire* Adrian Rance, 1988, 0 85263 957 0, 72pp; cover: cp Hampshire Farm Museum.

25. *Cumbria* John A. Nettleton, 1989, 0 85263 982 1, 64pp; cover: cp Grasmere by G. Blake.

26. *Norfolk* Margaret Knox, 1989, 0 85263 986 4, 72pp; cover: cp Wymondham market building.

27. *Devon* Peter Stanier, 1989, 0 85263 983 X, 96pp; cover: cp clapper bridge at Postbridge.

28. *Lancashire* John Champness, 1989, 0 85263 984 8, 64pp; cover: cp St George's Quay, Lancaster, by the author.

29. *Leicestershire and Rutland* Jeffery Hopewell, 1989, 0 85263 985 6, 68pp; cover: cp Normanton Church Water Museum, Rutland Water.

30. *Northumberland and Newcastle upon Tyne* Priscilla Boniface and Peter Fowler, 1989, 0 85263 998 8, 64pp; cover: cp Warkworth Castle.

31. *Glamorgan* John B. Hilling, 1991, 0 7478 0109 6, 80pp; cover: cp Castell Coch.

32. *Gloucestershire* Peter Stanier, 1991, 0 7478 0110 X, 80pp; cover: cp Arlington Row, Bibury.

33. *Gwynedd* Lawrence Garner, 1991, 0 7478 0111 8, 80pp; cover: cp Harlech Castle.

Shire Egyptology

Originally suggested by Ashley Jones of The Museum Bookshop, Great Russell Street, London WC1, this series was begun in 1984 under the editorship of Barbara Adams, Curator of the Petrie Museum of Egyptian Archaeology. This A5 (210 mm by 150 mm) square-backed series uses the same basic cover design as Shire Archaeology, with uniform typefaces, the title on each book printed in blue above a full-colour rectangular illustration. The series was numbered from the beginning, the numbers appearing only on the spines.

1. *Egyptian Mummies* Barbara Adams, 1984, 0 85263 699 7, 64pp; cover: cp Ptolemaic mummy of a woman. 4800 copies. 2nd ed, 1988, 0 85263 944 9.

2. *Egyptian Gods and Myths* Angela P. Thomas, 1986, 0 85263 788 8, 64pp; cover: oil painting 'The Gods and Their Makers' by Edwin Long. 4800 copies. Reprinted.

3. *Egyptian Painting and Relief* Gay Robins, 1986, 0 85263 789 6, 64pp; cover: painting from tomb of Tuthmosis IV. 4900 copies. Reprinted.

4. *Egyptian Textiles* Rosalind Hall, 1986, 0 85263 800 0, 72pp; cover: painting from tomb of Sennudjem. 4800 copies. Reprinted.

5. *Egyptian Pottery* Colin Hope, 1987, 0 85263 852 3, 64pp; cover: cp statuette of potter.

6. *Egyptian Pyramids and Mastaba Tombs* Philip Watson, 1987, 0 85263 853 1, 64pp; cover: cp Step Pyramid at Saqqara. 5000 copies. Reprinted.

7. *Predynastic Egypt* Barbara Adams, 1988, 0 85263 938 4, 76pp, cover: cp pottery bowl with hippopotami around rim.

8. *Egyptian Towns and Cities* Eric P. Uphill, 1988, 0 85263 939 2, 72pp; cover: cp Deir el-Medina village.

9. *Egyptian Food and Drink* Hilary Wilson, 1988, 0 85263 972 4, 64pp; cover: painting after relief in temple of Seti I by the author.

10. *Akhenaten's Egypt* Angela P. Thomas, 1988, 0 85263 973 2, 68pp; cover: painting of Akhenaten and family on modern papyrus.

11. *Egyptian Coffins* John H. Taylor, 1989, 0 85263 977 5, 68pp; cover: cp coffin of Nesperennub.

12. *Egyptian Household Animals* Rosalind and Jack Janssen, 1989, 0 7478 0000 6, 68pp; cover: cp tile depicting man leading a hound.

13. *Egyptian Metalworking and Tools* Bernd Scheel, 1989, 0 7478 0001 4, 68pp; cover: painting of metalworkers from tomb of Vizier Rekhmire.

14. *Egyptian Rock-cut Tombs* Aidan Dodson, 1991, 0 7478 0128 2, 64pp; cover: print of tombs of Beni Hasan by Lepsius.

Shire Natural History

This was the first Shire series to be illustrated in colour. First published in 1985, under the series editorship of Jim Flegg and Chris Humphries, these books fill the gap between general natural history compendia and full-length monographs. Each deals with an individual species or group of species, written by expert researchers and illustrated by some of the best wildlife photographers. They are all A5 format (210 mm by 150 mm), saddle-stitched with two wires, 24 pages in extent, illustrated with full colour and monochrome photographs, drawings and diagrams. The antler logo and cover design were by Megan Arnold. On a white cover a portrait colour photograph appears below a coloured title panel, with typefaces common to all books in the series. The series number appears on the spine and title page.

1. *Hawk-moths of the British Isles* Michael Easterbrook, 1985, 0 85263 743 8; cover: cp poplar hawk-moth by D. Chambers.

2. *The Puffin* Jim Flegg, 1985, 0 85263 744 6; cover: cp puffins by the author.

3. *Bee Orchids* Stephen Blackmore, 1985, 0 85263 745 4; cover: cp bee orchid by P. Lund.

4. *Fungi* Pamela Forey, 1985, 0 85263 746 2; cover: cp sulphur tuft by Tony Mundell.

5. *Parasitic Worms* Jim Flegg, 1985, 0 85263 761 6; cover: cp aphelenchoides attacking fungal mycelium.

6. *Buttercups* Stephen Blackmore, 1985, 0 85263 763 2; cover: cp creeping buttercup by the author.

7. *The Starling* C. J. Feare, 1985, 0 85263 764 0; cover: cp adult male starling by the author.

8. *Willows of the British Isles* Theresa Brendell, 1985, 0 85263 765 9; cover: cp male catkins of the dark-leaved willow by the author.

9. *Gorse* C. J. Humphries and E. Shaughnessy, 1987, 0 85263 810 8; cover: cp common gorse at Loch Ine by Heather Angel.

10. *Lichens* Jack R. Laundon, 1986, 0 85263 811 6; cover: cp lichen-covered headstone by the author.

11. *The Kingfisher* David Boag, 1986, 0 85263 831 0; cover: cp kingfisher by the author.

12. *The Swallow* Peter Tate, 1986, 0 85263 832 9; cover: cp female swallow in flight by Eric and David Hosking.

13. *The Blackbird* David W. Snow, 1987, 0 85263 854 X; cover: cp male blackbird singing by Eric and David Hosking.

14. *The Lapwing* Peter Weaver, 1987, 0 85263 855 8; cover: cp female lapwing incubating by Roger Wilmshurst.

15. *Bats of the British Isles* A. A. Wardhaugh, 1987, 0 85263 856 6; cover: cp Leisler's bat by S. Bisserot. Reprinted.

16. *The Sparrowhawk* Ian Newton, 1987, 0 85263 857 4; cover: cp male sparrowhawk at plucking post by R. J. C. Blewitt.

17. *The Blue Tit* Jim Flegg, 1987, 0 85263 716 0; cover: cp blue tit at nest entrance by John Hawkins.

18. *The Adder* Peter Stafford, 1987, 0 85263 879 5; cover: cp male adder by the author.

19. *Butterflies of the British Isles: The Nymphalidae* Michael Easterbrook, 1987, 0 85263 880 9; cover: cp small tortoiseshell and painted lady on buddleia by the author.

20. *The Brown Hare* Stephen Tapper, 1987, 0 85263 881 7; cover: cp two hares 'boxing' by Silvestris-Meyers.

21. *Ants of the British Isles* Gary J. Skinner, 1987, 0 85263 896 5; cover: cp red ant workers by the author.

22. *Longhorn Beetles of the British Isles* Norman Hickin, 1987, 0 85263 897 3; cover: cp *Callidium violaceum*, adult beetle by the author.

23. *The Cuckoo* Ian Wyllie, 1987, 0 85263 898 1; cover: cp female cuckoo removing egg by the author.

24. *Butterflies of the British Isles: The Lycaenidae* Michael Easterbrook, 1988, 0 85263 945 7; cover: cp male Adonis blue by Phil Chapman.

25. *Grasshoppers and Bush-crickets of the British Isles* Andrew Mahon, 1988, 0 85263 946 5; cover: cp common field grasshopper by the author.

26. *The Grey Seal* Sheila Anderson, 1988, 0 85263 947 3; cover: cp two female grey seals by the author.

27. *The Mute Swan* Janet Kear, 1988, 0 85263 948 1; cover: cp female mute swan and cygnet on nest by Roger Hosking.

28. *The Oystercatcher* Desmond Nethersole-Thompson, 1988, 0 85263 949 X; cover: cp oystercatcher and eggs by Eric and David Hosking.

29. *The Pheasant* P. A. Robertson, 1988, 0 85263 950 3; cover: cp cock pheasant guarding a hen by the author.

30. *Shrews of the British Isles* Sara Churchfield, 1988, 0 85263 951 1; cover: cp common shrew in its burrow by David Hosking.

31. *The Dipper* Stephanie J. Tyler and Stephen J. Ormerod, 1988 0 85263 955 4; cover: cp dipper by Roger Hosking.

32. *The Hedgehog* P. A. Morris, 1988, 0 85263 958 9; cover: cp head of male hedgehog by the author.

33. *The Redshank* W. G. Hale, 1988, 0 85263 959 7; cover: cp redshank settling on eggs by Eric and David Hosking.

34. *The Avocet* David Hill, 1989, 0 7478 0016 2; cover: cp avocet at rest by Chris Gomersall.

35. *The Common Seal* Paul Thompson, 1989, 0 7478 0017 0; cover: cp common seal group by the author.

36. *The Gannet* Bryan Nelson, 1989, 0 7478 0018 9; cover: cp gannet and chick by the author.

37. *The Great Crested Grebe* K. E. L. Simmons, 1989, 0 7478 0019 7; cover: cp adult great crested grebe by Jan van der Kam.

38. *Primulas of the British Isles* John Richards, 1989, 0 7478 0020 0; cover: cp primroses by the author.

39. *The Rabbit* Michael Leach, 1989, 0 7478 0021 9; cover: cp young rabbits in warren by the author.

40. *The Red Squirrel* Jessica Holm, 1989, 0 7478 0022 7; cover: cp red squirrel with chestnut by Eric and David Hosking.

41. *The Song Thrush* Eric Simms, 1989, 0 7478 0023 5; cover: cp song thrush and young in nest by Roger Wilmshurst.

42. *The Barn Owl* Iain R. Taylor, 1989, 0 7478 0024 3; cover: cp facial disk of barn owl by Eric and David Hosking. Reprinted.

43. *The Blackcap and the Garden Warbler* Ernest Garcia, 1989, 0 7478 0025 1; cover: cp male blackcap on nest by John Hawkins.

44. *Grasses* Patricia Hawley, 1989, 0 7478 0026 X; cover: cp smooth meadow grass by Stephen Blackmore.

45. *Land Snails of the British Isles* A. A. Wardhaugh, 1989, 0 7478 0027 8; cover: cp copse snail by the author.

46. *Lizards of the British Isles* Peter Stafford, 1989, 0 7478 0028 6; cover: cp male sand lizard by the author.

47. *Newts of the British Isles* Patrick J. Wisniewski, 1989, 0 7478 0029 4; cover: cp male smooth newt by G. Kinns.

48. *The Nightjar* Peter Tate, 1989, 0 7478 0030 8; cover: cp nightjar and sunset by Frank V. Blackburn.

49. *Umbellifers of the British Isles* Sabina Knees, 1989, 0 7478 0031 6; cover cp giant hogweed by the author.

50. *Butterflies of the British Isles: The Pieridae* Michael Easterbrook, 1989, 0 7478 0031 6; cover: cp male orange tip by David Chambers.

51. *The Barnacle Goose* Myrfyn Owen, 1990, 0 7478 0053 7; cover: cp barnacle goose by Joe Blossom.

52. *The Kestrel* Gordon Riddle, 1990, 0 7478 0054 5; cover: cp male kestrel with vole by the author.

53. *The Mandarin Duck* Christopher Lever, 1990, 0 7478 0055 3; cover: cp drake mandarin duck by R. Van Nostrand.

54. *Mice of the British Isles* Michael Leach, 1990, 0 7478 0056 1; cover: cp harvest mice by the author.

55. *The Curlew* Gerry Cotter, 1990 0 7478 0090 1; cover: cp curlew by J. C. Leedal.

56. *The Golden Eagle* John Love and Jeff Watson, 1990, 0 7478 0091 X; cover: cp head of immature golden eagle by J. A. Love.

57. *Harriers of the British Isles* Roger Clark, 1990, 0 7478 0092 8; cover: cp male hen harrier by S. Redpath.

58. *Poplars of the British Isles* Theresa Brendell, 1990, 0 7478 0093 6; cover: cp male catkins of black poplar by E. H. Herbert.

SHIRE ETHNOGRAPHY

The late Bryan Cranstone, formerly curator of the Pitt Rivers Museum in Oxford, was approached to develop this series on native cultures, their artefacts and customs, for students of ethnography but also for readers who had no specialist knowledge. The first title appeared in 1985. Shire Ethnography books are A5 format (210 mm x 150 mm), square-backed with spines, of varying length, with covers similar in design to Shire Archaeology and Shire Egyptology, a white ground with the title printed in red above a usually rectangular colour photograph. The series number appears only on the spine, above the mask logo.

1. *Indonesian Textile Techniques* Michael Hitchcock, 1985, 0 85263 769 1, 56pp; cover: cp Biman body-tension loom.

2. *Eskimo Carving* Susan M. Pearce, 1985, 0 85263 770 5, 64pp; cover: cp ivory harpoon rest in the form of two polar bears by Bruce Sinclair.

3. *Beads and Beadwork of East and South Africa* Margret Carey, 1986, 0 85263 797 7, 64pp; cover: cp Maasai disc necklet.

4. *The Algonquin Birchbark Canoe* David Gidmark, 1988, 0 85263 940 6, 64pp; cover: cp birchbark canoe on lake by the author.

5. *Art and Decoration of Central New Guinea* Barry Craig, 1988, 0 85263 941 4, 72pp; cover: cp Tifalmin cult house by the author.

6. *Textiles of the Kuna Indians of Panama* Herta Puls, 1988, 0 85263 942 2, 72pp; cover: cp mola by the author.

7. *Polynesian Barkcloth* Simon Kooijman, 1988, 0 85263 943 0, 64pp; cover: cp beating paper mulberry bark on Mothe Island by the author.

8. *Betel-chewing Equipment of East New Guinea* Harry Beran, 1988, 0 85263 969 4, 72pp; cover: cp two carved spatulas in the Museum of Mankind, London.

9. *Mexican Textile Techniques* Chloë Sayer, 1988, 0 85263 970 8, 64pp; cover: cp backstrap loom used by Trique Indians, by the author.

10. *Arts and Crafts of Torres Strait* David R. Moore, 1989, 0 7478 0007 3, 64pp; cover: cp turtleshell mask.

11. *Cassava and Chicha: Bread and Beer of the Amazonian Indians* Linda Mowat, 1989, 0 7478 0008 1, 64pp; cover: cp Tiriyo women grating manioc by Dr Peter Riviere.

12. *Chikan Embroidery: The Floral Whitework of India* Sheila Paine, 1989, 0 7478 0009 X, 60pp; cover: cp kurtha from Lucknow by Sue Ormerod.

13. *Ibo Art* G. I. Jones, 1989, 0 7478 0012 X, 72pp; cover: cp helmet mask from Amobia by the author.

14. *Malagasy Textiles* John Mack, 1989, 0 7478 0015 4, 60pp; cover: painting of Merina woman weaving on single-heddle loom, by artist Rainimaharosoa.

15. *Peruvian Pottery* George Bankes, 1989, 0 7478 0013 8, 72pp; cover: cp spout and handle bottle.

16. *Peruvian Textiles* Jane Feltham, 1989, 0 7478 0014 6, 72pp; cover: cp woman weaving on backstrap loom by Rosalie Gotch.

17. *Crafts and Traditions of the Canary Islands* Mike Eddy, 1989, 0 7478 0011 1, 68pp; cover: cp basketry workshop.

18. *Cook Islands Art* Dale Idiens, 1990, 0 7478 0061 8, 64pp; cover: cp fisherman's god by Ken Smith.

19. *Metalcrafts of Central Asia* Ken Teague, 1990, 0 7478 0062 6, 64 pp; cover: cp brass plaque from Mongolia by the author.

20. *Polynesian Sound-producing Instruments* Richard Moyle, 1990, 0 7478 0095 2, 64pp; cover: cp nose-flute players in Tonga by Luis Marden.

21. *Beads and Beadwork of West and Central Africa* Margret Carey, 1991, 0 7478 0100 2, 56pp; cover: cp Yoruba beadwork model of three figures.

Shire Garden History

Launched in 1988 with three titles, this A5, square-backed series was the second to use colour illustrations in the text. The tree tub logo and cover title panel design were by Megan Arnold. The series numbers appear on the spine and verso.

1. *Restoring Period Gardens* John Harvey, 1988, 0 85263 952 X, 112pp; cover: cp Nash's garden at Brighton Pavilion.

2. *Florists' Flowers and Societies* Ruth Duthie, 1988, 0 85263 953 8, 96pp; cover: water-colour of mixed flowers by Thomas Robins the elder, 1768.

3. *The English Landscape Garden* Miles Hadfield, 1977, 0 85263 345 9, 72pp; cover: photo Stourhead, green and black. 4000 copies. First published as a non-series title. 2nd ed, 1988, 0 85263 919 8; cover: cp Temple of the Four Winds at Castle Howard. Reissued as part of the Shire Garden History series.

4. *The Renaissance Garden in Britain* John Anthony, 1991, 0 7478 0130 4, 96pp; cover: cp Powys Castle.

5. *The English Rococo Garden* Michael Symes, 1991, 0 7478 0129 0, 72pp; cover: water-colour 'The Garden at Woodside, Old Windsor', by Thomas Robins the elder, *c*.1750.

Gothick Guides

These gazetteers of the myths, mysteries, spectres, superstitions, crimes and calamities of each county are A5 format (210 mm by 150 mm), square-backed with spines, of varying length, and with a cover illustration by Grahame Tomkins common to all titles in the series. The series number is given on the verso.

1. *Gothick Hertfordshire* Jennifer Westwood, 1989, 0 7478 0041 3, 52pp.
2. *Gothick Norfolk* Jennifer Westwood, 1989, 0 7478 0042 1, 48pp.

Non-series titles

Although Shire has published most of its books as part of series, it has occasionally produced individual titles or small groups of titles issued together that are outside the established series. These are described here in chronological order of publication.

Zoos, Bird Gardens and Animal Collections in Great Britain and Eire Kate Bergamar, 1969, 0 85263 066 2, 177mm by 113 mm, 72pp, spined; cover: ld elephant, giraffe, lion, peacock, goose by Edward Stamp, red and black. 5000 copies. 2nd ed, 1970, 0 85263 093 X, 64pp; cover change: yellow and black.

The Road to the Costa Brava Eric Whelpton, 1969, 0 85263 029 8, 177 mm by 113 mm, 40pp, stitched; cover: ld scenes on route by Barbara Whelpton, orange and black. 2100 copies.

The Road to Provence Eric Whelpton, 1969, 0 85263 030 1, 177 mm by 113 mm, 40pp, stitched; cover: ld scenes on route by Barbara Whelpton, lime and black. 2400 copies.

The Road to Rome via Florence Eric Whelpton, 1969, 0 85263 031 X, 177 mm by 113 mm, 48pp, stitched; cover: ld scenes on route by Barbara Whelpton, blue and black. 2200 copies.

The Road to Rome via Genoa Eric Whelpton, 1969, 0 85263 032 8, 177 mm by 113 mm, 48pp, stitched; cover: ld scenes on route by Barbara Whelpton, ochre and black. 1900 copies.

The Road to Salzburg Eric Whelpton, 1969, 0 85263 033 6, 177 mm by 113 mm, 48pp, stitched; cover: ld scenes on route by Barbara Whelpton, pink and black. 2000 copies.

The Road to Venice Eric Whelpton, 1969, 0 85263 034 4, 177 mm by 113 mm, 40pp, stitched; cover: ld scenes on route by Barbara Whelpton, purple and black. 2100 copies.

Stap Me! The British Newspaper Strip Denis Gifford, 1971, A5, 96pp, spined; cover: ld 'Jane' and 'Just Jake' design by the author, green orange and black. 4000 copies. 1974, remaining stock rebound in new cover: *The History of the British Newspaper Comic Strip*, design by Ron Shaddock, grey and black.

The Complete Zodiac Entertainer Margaret M. Pearson, 1973, 0 85994 000 4, 185 mm by 120 mm, 96pp, hardbacked with dust jacket; jacket: ld Zodiac-headed party-goers by Ron Shaddock, orange yellow pink and black. 3000 copies. Published under the imprint Cadbury Lamb at Aylesbury address.

Non-series titles

The Vampyre John William Polidori, introduction by Russell Ash, 1974, 0 85263 244 4, octavo vi+42pp, hardbacked with printed boards; cover: pattern of moon and vampire by Bernard Crossland Associates, blue yellow and black. 1000 copies. Published under the imprint The Gubblecote Press, Tring, Hertfordshire.

The Early Barrow Diggers Barry M. Marsden, 1974, 0 85263 242 8, octavo x+126pp, hardbacked with dust jacket; jacket: engraving barrow-opening, design by Robin Ollington, blue brown and black. 2500 copies. Published as part of the Folk Life Library with corn dolly colophon on spine.

Complete Book of Home Entertainment Gyles Brandreth, 1974, 0 85263 267 3, A5, 222pp, spined; cover: ld rabbit and top hat by Ron Shaddock, blue brown and black. 3000 copies.

Keys — Their History and Collection Eric Monk, 1974, 0 85263 254 1, A5, 64pp, spined; cover: ld keys on keyring by Ron Shaddock, black pink and grey. 2900 copies. 1983; new cover: cp group of old keys.

From Antiquary to Archaeologist Robert H. Cunnington, 1975, 0 85263 265 7, octavo xviii+178pp, hardbacked with dust jacket; jacket: watercolour of barrow-opening by Philip Crocker, design by Ron Shaddock, brown and black. 1000 copies. Published as part of the Folk Life Library with corn dolly colophon on spine.

Hedgerow Plants Molly Hyde, 1976, 0 85263 331 9, A5, 192pp, spined; cover: ld flowers by the author, design by Ron Shaddock, olive yellow and black. 3000 copies.

The English Landscape Garden Miles Hadfield. See Shire Garden History.

Having a Baby Margaret Leonard, 1977, 0 85263 385 8, 180 mm by 110 mm, 96pp, spined; cover: cp young couple by M. Bass. 15,000 copies. Family Care book 1.

Your Baby's Early Days Margaret Leonard, 1977, 0 85263 386 6, 180 mm by 110 mm, 96pp, spined; cover: cp mother and baby by M. Bass. 8000 copies. Family Care book 2.

Nearly One Year Old Margaret Leonard, 1977, 0 85263 387 4, 180 mm by 110 mm, 96pp, spined; cover: cp baby with toys by M. Bass. 6000 copies. Family Care book 3.

Becoming a Toddler Margaret Leonard, 1977, 0 85263 388 2, 180 mm by 110 mm, 96pp, spined; cover: cp boy with baby walker by M. Bass. 6000 copies. Family Care book 4.

Modelling Farm Carts John Vince, 1977, 0 85263 405 6, A5, 48pp, stitched; cover: cp model dung cart. 5000 copies. 2nd ed, 1979, 0 85263 482 X. Shire Modelmaker number 1.

Modelling Farm Wagons John Vince, 1977, 0 85263 406 4, A5, 48pp, stitched; cover: cp model Sussex wagon. 5000 copies. 2nd ed, 1979, 0 85263 483 8. Shire Modelmaker number 2.

Elementary Surveying for Industrial Archaeologists Hugh Bodey and Michael Hallas, 1977, 0 85263 375 0, A5, 64pp, spined; cover: ld building plan, grey and carmine. 2700 copies.

Keeping a Donkey Dorothy Morris, 1979, 0 85263 435 8, A5, 80pp, spined; cover: cp head of donkey. 4200 copies.

The Identification of Lace Pat Earnshaw, 1980, 0 85263 484 6, A5, 160pp, spined; cover: photo lace, black. 4900 copies. 2nd ed, 1984, 0 85263 701 2. The first edition is distinguished from reprints prior to 1984 only by the price £3.95 on the back cover. Reprints are priced £4.95.

Breadmaking and Yeast Cookery Doreen Chetwood, 1980, 0 85263 493 5, A5, 48pp, spined; cover: cp various breads. 4800 copies.

The Saddler Sidney A. Davis, 1980, 0 85263 573 3, A5, 64pp, spined; cover: cp author making a saddle. 3900 copies.

A Dictionary of Lace Pat Earnshaw, 1982, 0 85263 602 4, A5, 240pp, spined; cover: photo lace, purple. 4500 copies. 2nd ed, 1984, 0 85263 700 4.

Old Jewellery Duncan James, 1989, 0 7478 0047 2, A5, 100pp, spined; cover: cp Victorian necklace, earrings and brooches.

Medieval Wall Paintings E. Clive Rouse, 1991, 0 7478 0144 4, A5, 80pp, spined; cover: watercolour King David, Longthorpe Tower, by the author. See *Discovering Wall Paintings*, no. 22 in the 'Discovering' series.

The Organ David Baker, 1991, 0 7478 0131 2, A5, 80pp, spined; cover: cp organ, Wymondham parish church by Tony Freeman-Cosh.

Shire archive

St Albans Richard Tames, 1973, 0 85263 159 6. A wallet (225 mm by 345 mm) of 25 loose documents with contents sheets relating the history of St Albans. Grey board printed black. 2000 copies.

Shire postcards

These reproductions of old engravings were first published in 1975, printed in one colour on a cast-coated, one-sided art board, 100 mm by 145 mm, in sets of varying numbers. Each bears the Shire address, series number and title, card number, subject and source.

1. *Rural Industry in Early Nineteenth Century Britain.* Illustrations from *Microcosm* 1806 by W. H. Pyne. 1975, sepia, 10 cards.

2. *Victorian Farming.* Illustrations from *Book of the Farm* 1890 by Stephens. 1975, dark brown, 10 cards.

3. *Old Fashioned Christmas.* Illustrations from *Illustrated London News*, etc. 1975, crimson, 6 cards.

4. *Gilbert and Sullivan.* Illustrations from *Songs of a Savoyard* by W. S. Gilbert. 1975, black, 12 cards.

5. *Old Carts and Wagons.* Illustrations from *Microcosm* 1806 by W. H. Pyne, etc. 1975, sepia, 6 cards.

6. *Bewick's Dogs.* Illustrations from *A General History of Quadrupeds* 1824 by Thomas Bewick. 1976, black, 6 cards.

7. *Agriculture in Early Nineteenth Century Britain.* Illustrations from *Microcosm* 1806 by W. H. Pyne. 1976, brown, 6 cards.

8. *Corn Dollies.* Illustrations by R. C. Lambeth. 1976, black on straw-coloured background, 6 cards.

9. *Shire Cartoons.* Illustrations by Larry, Hector Breeze, Honeysett etc. 1979, black, 6 cards. Published for and distributed at the Booksellers Association Conference.

10. *Cartoons.* Illustrations by Bill Tidy. 1981, black, 4 cards, 185 mm by 120 mm. Published for and distributed at the Museums Association Conference, Manchester, 1981.

Shire Postcard Games. From *Discovering Old Board Games.* Nine Men's Morris, Fox and Geese. 1976, brown, 2 cards.

SHIRE WARGAMING STATIONERY

Pads of printed white cartridge, 230 mm by 180 mm; 50 sheets, with illustrated cover and instructions for use, black on coloured stock. 1972.

SW1 Map movement order sheets. 1000 pads.
SW2 Wargame order sheets. 1000 pads.
SW3 18th century naval warfare signal logs. 500 pads.
SW4 18th century naval warfare scoring plans. 500 pads.

CHILTERN SOCIETY FOOTPATH MAPS

The Chiltern Society was founded by Christopher Hall and Ted Castle in 1965 and the Society's Rights of Way Group was set up to protect and restore public rights of way in the Chilterns. To this end it issued, in June 1969, a map of footpaths around Marlow, on the reverse of which were descriptions of local walks. A second map, of Henley NW, followed the next year and by 1972 the Society had five in the series.

In 1972 Don Gresswell, the Honorary Secretary of the Rights of Way Group, persuaded Shire Publications to take over publication of the maps, whereby the cartography and text for the maps would be supplied free by volunteers and royalties on sales would go to the Chiltern Society. Originally several cartographers were involved but standardisation began in 1978 and since 1982 all mapping has been done by Bill Chester from information supplied by Nick Moon. Rights of way particulars are updated each time a new edition is published.

The maps, drawn to a scale of $2^1/_2$ inches to 1 mile, are a single sheet of strong stock folded into four, 203 mm x 134 mm. The first map was printed in black only on both sides. From no. 2 to no. 10 the words 'The Chiltern Society' were printed in green on the front. In 1976 this was changed to a design of stile, fence and fingerpost by Bill Chester, printed in blue, green and black, the text and map remaining black. All maps bear the beech tree logo of the Chiltern Society and are numbered although the titles of some maps were changed in the 1980s to identify better the towns that each covers. From 1986 International Standard Book Numbers were printed on the backs of the maps.

1. *Marlow and district,* 1969, black, published by Chiltern Society. 2nd ed, 1970, black and green. 3rd ed, 1972, published by Shire. 4th ed, 1974. 5th ed, 1978, new cover blue green and black. 6th ed, *High Wycombe and Marlow,* 1984. 7th ed, 1987, 0 85263 813 2. 8th ed, 1990, 0 7478 0102 9.

2. *Henley NW,* 1970, black and green, published by Chiltern Society. Reprinted. 2nd ed, 1972, published by Shire. 3rd ed, *Henley North West,* 1977, new cover blue green and black. 4th ed, *Henley and Nettlebed,* 1984. 5th ed, 1987, 0 85263 814 0. 6th ed, 1991, 0 7478 0132 0.

3. *Wendover and district,* 1971, black and green, published by Chiltern Society and Wendover Society. 2nd ed, 1972, published by Shire. 3rd ed, 1974. 4th ed, 1977, new cover blue green and black. 5th ed, 1979. 6th ed, *Wendover and Princes Risborough,* 1985. 7th ed, 1990, 0 7478 0122 3. Incorrectly reads 'Eighth edition'.

4. *Henley SW,* 1971, black and green, published by Chiltern Society. Reprinted, 1974, published by Shire. 2nd ed, *Henley Southwest,* 1979, new cover blue green and black. 3rd ed, *Henley and Caversham,* 1984. 4th ed, 1988, 0 85263 816 7.

5. *Sarratt and Chipperfield,* 1971, black and green, published by the Chiltern Society. 2nd ed, 1973, published by Shire. 3rd ed, 1977, new cover blue green and black. 4th ed, 1983. 5th ed, 1987, 0 85263 817 5. 6th ed, 1991, 0 7478 0146 0.

6. *The Penn Country,* 1972, black and green, published by Shire. 2nd ed, 1975. 3rd ed, 1979, new cover blue green and black. 4th ed, *Amersham and the Penn Country,* 1984. 5th ed, 1986, 0 85263 818 3. 6th ed, 1988, 0 85263 976 7. Incorrectly reads 'Fourth edition'. 7th ed, 1991, 0 7478 0147 9.

7. *Wycombe NW,* 1972, black and green. Oversize with additional fold. 2nd ed, *Wycombe Northwest,* 1977, new cover blue green and black. Remapped to standard format. 3rd ed, 1981. Map reads 1977 but location map on back identifies this edition. 4th ed, *West Wycombe and Princes Risborough,* 1985. 5th ed, 1991, 0 7478 0145 2.

8. *Chartridge and Cholesbury,* 1973, black and green. 2nd ed, 1977, new cover blue green and black. 3rd ed, 1983. 4th ed, 1987, 0 85263 820 5.

9. *The Oxfordshire Escarpment,* 1974, black and green. 2nd ed, 1975. 3rd ed, 1980, new cover blue green and black. 4th ed, 1985. 5th ed, 1989, 0 85263 821 3. Incorrectly reads 'Fourth edition'.

10. *Ewelme and district,* 1975, black and green. 2nd ed, 1979, new cover blue green and black. 3rd ed, *Wallingford and Watlington,* 1986, 0 85263 822 1.

11. *The Hambleden Valley,* 1976, blue green and black. 2nd ed, 1979. 3rd ed, 1984. 4th ed, 1987, 0 85263 823 X. 5th ed, 1990, 0 7478 0101 0.

12. *The Hughenden Valley,* 1978, blue green and black. 2nd ed, *Hughenden Valley and Great Missenden,* 1985. 3rd ed, 1987, 0 85263 824 8. 4th ed, 1991, 0 7478 0134 7.

13. *Beaconsfield and district,* 1980, blue green and black. 2nd ed, 1984. 3rd ed, 1987, 0 85263 825 6.

14. *Stokenchurch and district,* 1980, blue green and black. 2nd ed, *Stokenchurch and Chinnor,* 1985.

15. *Crowmarsh and Nuffield,* 1981, blue green and black. 2nd ed, 1986, 0 85263 827 2.

16. *Goring and Mapledurham,* 1981, blue green and black. 2nd ed, 1985.

17. *Chesham and Berkhamsted,* 1981, blue green and black. 2nd ed, 1984. 3rd ed, 1987, 0 85263 829 9. 4th ed, 1991, 0 7478 0133 9.

18. *Tring and district,* 1981, blue green and black. 2nd ed, *Tring and Wendover,* 1984. 3rd ed, 1986, 0 85263 830 2. 4th ed, 1989, 0 7478 0077 4.

19. *Ivinghoe and Ashridge,* 1988, blue green and black, 0 85263 956 2. Reprinted, 1989.

Walks in the Hertfordshire Chilterns Nick Moon, 1986, 0 85263 690 3, 40pp; cover: map design of stile, fence and finger post, blue green and black.

THE COVER ARTISTS

ROSALIE BULLOCK

Rosalie Bullock studied textile design at the Royal College of Art and since then has worked as a freelance textile and graphic designer. In 1986 she began painting seriously and in 1987 had her first one-person show at the Tradescant Garden Museum in London. Other exhibitions followed. Since then many of her paintings have been reproduced as greetings cards and prints. She is presently working on a book on the subject of the painter in the garden.

ROBIN OLLINGTON

Apart from two years in the Army (with the nickname Rembrandt) Robin Ollington has been engaged in art, advertising and design all his working life. Trained at Lowestoft School of Art, where he later joined the staff, he has been involved in many aspects of design from packaging and advertising to illustration, theatre and exhibition work.

He has spent the last twenty five years in advertising, as a director and a creative director in London agencies. He has undertaken commissions for a variety of clients, organisations and projects ranging from the design of the Beatrix Potter Exhibition at the Tate Gallery to a set of postage stamps issued in 1992 to celebrate the 500th anniversary of the discovery of America. During his long association with Shire Publications he designed over 55 covers.

Robin's leisure interests also lead to creative involvement. As a member of SAVE Britain's Heritage he has produced well over 50 report and book covers whilst his designs for church and charity mugs, brochures and tea towels are continuously in demand!

FELIX PARTRIDGE

Born in January 1923 without apparent creative genius, Felix Partridge was nevertheless dispatched to art school at the age of thirteen. He first attended Blackheath School of Art and then Goldsmith's College, until the Second World War when he served without distinction as a sapper.

There followed three years at the Royal College of Art discovering the arcane pleasures of stained glass and marriage. The advent of a family, two sons and a daughter, brought a decision to leave London for what was then rural Bedfordshire, commuting daily to various sources of work: teaching, freelance illustration, advertising and publishing. Painting remained a luxury. Felix later ran a very successful summer school in south-west France with his wife Monique, a talented illustrator and watercolourist. Now, fifteen years on, it is time to relax with friends and paint.

RON SHADDOCK

Ron Shaddock began his career in a London commercial art studio as a trainee in 1955, following two years of National Service in the RAF. After three years he moved on to the creative studio of the Decca Record Company on the Albert Embankment to design record sleeves, point of sale material and Decca's record magazine. Three years later he joined a Watford-based design group where he stayed for ten years before leaving to work as a freelance designer. He has worked from his Tring base since the early 1970s, producing designs and artwork for book jackets, brochures, stationery, exhibition panels and company newspapers for a variety of clients.

The cover artists

MIKE SMITH

Although born in Surrey, the youngest of five children, Mike Smith has spent most of his life in Hertfordshire and Buckinghamshire. After attending first Ealing and then Watford Art College he began his career as a graphic artist with John Dickinsons in Apsley. He was an active member of the Hemel Hempstead Cycling Club and at eighteen became their Junior Champion. Following National Service in the RAF Mike became publicity manager with Access Equipment Limited, an engineering company in Hemel Hempstead, and later joined the office equipment firm Rexel Limited in Aylesbury as sales promotion manager.

Mike now runs his own company from an office in Tring, trading as Gemini Design and Advertising, which offers a service to local businesses. In 1991 he was a winner in a national design competition run by Sappi Graphics of Nash Mills. Strangely, the company now run by Sappi Graphics was for many years called John Dickinsons.

EDWARD STAMP

Born in London in 1939, Edward Stamp was evacuated during the war to a small farm in Dunton, Buckinghamshire. In 1961 he gained the National Diploma of Design at the Northampton School of Art and a period of commercial work and freelance book illustration followed. He subsequently became leading illustrator with Her Majesty's Stationery Office. Yet he could not resist the lure of the countryside and left his urban office life to work on the land.

He happily combined the life of farming with that of an artist until 1970. During this period he designed many covers for Shire books and illustrated several with line drawings. The appreciation of his work at a number of provincial one-man exhibitions led him to devote more time to painting and in 1973 he first exhibited in London with such success that fine art became his full-time career. In 1980 he was awarded the Bronze Medal for the most outstanding watercolour by a non-member in the annual exhibition of the RA, and was elected a member. In 1981 his wood engravings earned him membership of the Royal Institute of Painters, Etchers and Engravers. His work has been shown regularly at the Royal Academy since 1975.

GRAHAME JAMES TOMKINS

Grahame James Tomkins was born in Marylebone, London, in 1939, but he has lived in Hemel Hempstead since 1947. He trained in art at Watford Technical College and then as a technical illustrator with a local engineering firm. During his National Service in the RAF from 1960 to 1962 he was a member of the RAF Exhibition Design and Display Unit at Hendon, where the RAF museum is situated.

Grahame's career has been in commercial art since then, and he specialises in personalised cartoons for retirements and other special occasions in the business world. Now a director of Clearway Arts Limited in Watford, he has exhibited his watercolours and oils at various exhibitions and has held a successful one-man show.

LIZ TRESILIAN

After studying art at the West of England College of Art Liz Tresilian worked as a reporter and feature writer with a group of newspapers and magazines based in Marlborough and Swindon. In 1967-8 she contributed some articles to *Bucks Life*, thus beginning her association with Shire Publications. She sold advertising on a new edition of *Discovering Norfolk* and then wrote *Discovering Wiltshire* and *Discovering Castle Combe*, where she was living at the time. Family commitments and running a design studio prevented her from continuing freelance work for some time, but she has had nine other books published.

ALPHABETICAL LISTING OF TITLES

Titles are listed alphabetically within each series, each with its series number. Refer back to the numerical listing for full information about a book.

'Discovering' books

'Discovering' books, continued

Lifelines

Shire Albums

Shire Albums, continued

History in Camera

Shire Archaeology

Shire Archaeology, continued

Romano-British Wall Painting 42
Roman Roads 10
Roman Villas 11
Samian Ware 55
Teaching Archaeology in Schools 29
Textiles in Archaeology 56
Towns in Roman Britain 13
Viking Age Archaeology 60
Village Plans 27
Villages in Roman Britain 49
Wood in Archaeology 17

Shire County Guides

Bedfordshire 12
Buckinghamshire 13
Cambridgeshire and Cambridge 23
Cheshire 17
Cornwall 14
Cumbria 25
Derbyshire and the Peak District 6
Devon 27
Dorset 9
Essex 10
Glamorgan 31
Gloucestershire 32
Gwent 15
Gwynedd 33
Hampshire 24
Herefordshire and the Black Mountains 16
Hertfordshire 18
Kent 19
Lancashire 28
Leicestershire and Rutland 29
Lincolnshire and South Humberside 2
Norfolk 26
Northamptonshire 22
Northumberland and Newcastle upon Tyne 30
North Yorkshire and North Humberside 3
Oxfordshire and Oxford 20
Shropshire 7
Somerset 1
Staffordshire 11
Surrey 8
Sussex 4
West Yorkshire 21
Wiltshire 5

Shire Egyptology

Akhenaten's Egypt 10
Egyptian Coffins 11
Egyptian Food and Drink 9
Egyptian Gods and Myths 2
Egyptian Household Animals 12
Egyptian Metalworking and Tools 13
Egyptian Mummies 1
Egyptian Painting and Relief 3
Egyptian Pottery 5
Egyptian Pyramids and Mastaba Tombs 6
Egyptian Rock-cut Tombs 14
Egyptian Textiles 4
Egyptian Towns and Cities 8
Predynastic Egypt 7

Shire Natural History

Adder, The 18
Ants of the British Isles 21
Avocet, The 34
Barnacle Goose, The 51
Barn Owl, The 42
Bats of the British Isles 15
Bee Orchids 3
Blackbird, The 13
Blackcap and Garden Warbler, The 43
Blue Tit, The 17
Brown Hare, The 20
Buttercups 6
Butterflies of the British Isles: The Lycaenidae 24
Butterflies of the British Isles: The Nymphalidae 19
Butterflies of the British Isles: The Pieridae 50
Common Seal, The 35
Cuckoo, The 23
Curlew, The 55
Dipper, The 31
Fungi 4
Gannet, The 36
Golden Eagle, The 56
Gorse 9
Grasses 44
Grasshoppers and Bush-crickets of the British Isles 25
Great Crested Grebe, The 37
Grey Seal, The 26
Harriers of the British Isles 57
Hawk-moths of the British Isles 1
Hedgehog, The 32
Kestrel, The 52
Kingfisher, The 11
Land Snails of the British Isles 45
Lapwing, The 14
Lichens 10
Lizards of the British Isles 46
Longhorn Beetles of the British Isles 22
Mandarin Duck, The 53
Mice of the British Isles 54
Mute Swan, The 27
Newts of the British Isles 47
Nightjar, The 48
Oystercatcher, The 28
Parasitic Worms 5
Pheasant, The 29
Poplars of the British Isles 58
Primulas of the British Isles 38
Puffin, The 2
Rabbit, The 39
Redshank, The 33
Red Squirrel, The 40
Shrews of the British Isles 30
Song Thrush, The 41
Sparrowhawk, The 16
Starling, The 7
Swallow, The 12
Umbellifers of the British Isles 49
Willows of the British Isles 8

Shire Ethnography

Algonquin Birchbark Canoe, The 4
Art and Decoration of Central New Guinea 5
Arts and Crafts of Torres Strait 10
Beads and Beadwork of East and South Africa 3
Beads and Beadwork of West and Central Africa 21
Betel-chewing Equipment of East New Guinea 8
Cassava and Chicha: Bread and Beer of the Amazonian Indians 11
Chikan Embroidery: The Floral Whitework of India 12
Cook Islands Art 18
Crafts and Traditions of the Canary Islands 17
Eskimo Carving 2
Ibo Art 13
Indonesian Textile Techniques 1
Malagasy Textiles 14
Metalcrafts of Central Asia 19
Mexican Textile Techniques 9
Peruvian Pottery 15
Peruvian Textiles 16
Polynesian Barkcloth 7
Polynesian Sound-producing Instruments 20
Textiles of the Kuna Indians of Panama 6

Shire Garden History

English Landscape Garden, The 3
English Rococo Garden, The 5
Florists' Flowers and Societies 2
Renaissance Garden in Britain, The 4
Restoring Period Gardens 1

Gothick Guides

Gothick Hertfordshire 1
Gothick Norfolk 2

Non-series titles

Becoming a Toddler
Breadmaking and Yeast Cookery
Complete Book of Home Entertainment
Complete Zodiac Entertainer, The
Dictionary of Lace, A
Early Barrow Diggers, The
Elementary Surveying for Industrial Archaeologists
English Landscape Garden, The
From Antiquary to Archaeologist
Having a Baby
Hedgerow Plants
History of the British Newspaper Comic Strip, The
Identification of Lace, The
Keeping a Donkey
Keys — Their History and Collection
Medieval Wall Paintings
Modelling Farm Carts
Modelling Farm Wagons
Nearly One Year Old
Old Jewellery
Organ, The
Road to Provence, The
Road to Rome via Florence, The
Road to Rome via Genoa, The
Road to Salzburg, The
Road to the Costa Brava, The
Road to Venice, The
Saddler, The
Stap Me! The British Newspaper Strip
Vampyre, The
Your Baby's Early Days
Zoos, Bird Gardens and Animal Collections in Great Britain and Eire

Chiltern Society Footpath Maps

Amersham and the Penn Country 6
Beaconsfield and District 13
Chartridge and Cholesbury 8
Chesham and Berkhamsted 17
Crowmarsh and Nuffield 15
Ewelme and District 10
Goring and Mapledurham 16
Hambleden Valley, The 11
Henley and Caversham 4
Henley and Nettlebed 2
Henley North West 2
Henley South West 4
High Wycombe and Marlow 1
Hughenden Valley, The 12
Hughenden Valley and Great Missenden 12
Ivinghoe and Ashridge 19
Marlow and District 1
Oxfordshire Escarpment 9
Penn Country, The 6
Sarratt and Chipperfield 5
Stokenchurch and Chinnor 14
Stokenchuch and District 14
Tring and District 18
Tring and Wendover 18
Walks in the Hertfordshire Chilterns (book)
Wallingford and Watlington 10
Wendover and District 3
Wendover and Princes Risborough 3
West Wycombe and Princes Risborough 7
Wycombe Northwest 7

GENERAL INDEX

A complete index of Shire publications listed in this book, with page references.

General index

General index

General index

General index

General index

General index

General index